The Life and Times of
EDWARD III

OVERLEAF LEFT A message of defiance from
Robert the Bruce to Edward III.
(Bibliothèque Nationale)
RIGHT English forces besiege a town in the
Hundred Years' War.
(Bibliothèque Nationale)

peut. Et tournoyerent. ij.
fois en celle belle saison a
condet.

Comment robert de breuv roy
descoce deffia le roy edouart
dangleterre. Le. vi.e chap.

The Life and Times of
EDWARD III

Paul Johnson

Introduction by Antonia Fraser

Weidenfeld and Nicolson
London

© Weidenfeld and Nicolson
and Book Club Associates 1973

Series design by Paul Watkins
Layout by Juanita Grout

Filmset by Keyspools Ltd, Lancashire
Printed in Great Britain by
Westerham Press Ltd, Westerham, Kent

Contents

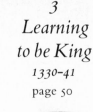

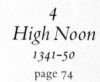

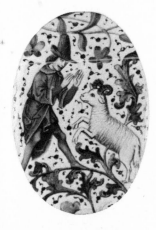

Introduction

Edward iii, that titan whose reign sprawls across fifty years of the fourteenth century – if one could pick one quality which sums up his character in its glorious prime, it would be, in Paul Johnson's striking phrase, his 'huge self-confidence' that he could work with the English nation as a whole. For it is inevitable that in our own age, our interest should focus on such relevant subjects as the growth of English nationalism in the Anglo-French struggle, or more important still, the exact relationship and division of authority between King and Parliament.

Was this not the era of Crécy, that great victory when English longbows of maple, oak and yew, penetrating even the chain-mail of the French kings, made the name of England splendid or at least unforgettable on the Continent? At the end of the day, after fifteen French charges, there were four thousand French knights dead, 'men of superior dignity' said Froissart; they included the King of Bohemia, from whose helmet Edward's son the Black Prince appropriated that famous motto *Ich Dien*. In this reign too the arts flourished harmoniously with the military virtues: it was symbolic that the Court orchestra became a military band in wartime, and what was more, at a slightly higher rate of pay. It was Edward iii who founded the Order of the Garter, in honour of the lovely Joan, Countess of Salisbury, according to a famous story which we are pleased to discover here may even have the ring of truth. English came to replace French as a vernacular language: this was the time of Wycliffe, *Sir Gawayne and the Grene Knight*, and Chaucer's *Canterbury Tales*, which, although written later, evoke that society which Edward iii produced.

Paul Johnson's achievement is to weld this diversity of social development and great events into the coherent story of a reign, and above all the biography of a man. What a magnificent son in his early years was this Edward, born of the pathetic Edward ii, and his Queen Isabella, paramour of Mortimer! But if we concentrate on the King himself, Edward's story must be seen in the end as 'a double tragedy'. The Black Death of 1348 onwards dissolved the society he had known, while the attrition of war made for example, the victory of Poitiers in 1356 less effective than that of Crécy ten years before. So the early domestic achievements too gave way to the degeneration consequent on old age, just as the happy fruitful marriage to Queen Philippa (twelve children ranging from the Black Prince to John of Gaunt) was replaced by the publicly less satisfying relationship with Alice Perrers. A strong-minded woman, who fought for her rights in a man's world, she has probably been unfairly blamed, because her dominance coincided with the weakness of an old man. What is incontrovertible is that the long reign – 1327-77 – ended in military reverses, and those in turn lead to political reverses. Nevertheless that in itself should not detract from the original brightness of this leonine king. It was perhaps inherent in the nature of fourteenth-century monarchy.

Antonia Fraser

Acknowledgments

Photographs and illustrations were supplied by and are reproduced by kind permission of the following: Batsford: 182–3, Bibliothèque Nationale: 2, 3, 10, *14-15*, 21, 28, 29, *33*, 42/1, 42/3, 68, 74-5, 88-9, *94-5*, 97, 98, 99, 101, 170-1, 173, *178-9*, 185, 202; Bibliothèque Royale Albert Ier, Brussels: *98*; Bodleian Library: 20/1, 20/2, *45*, 80-1/2, 100, 106, *110*, 116-7, 138-9, 142-3, 155, 156/1, 156/2, 167, 194; British Museum: 13, 17, 25, 34, 35, 38/2, 38/3, 42/2, 43/1, 43/3, 70, 80-1/1, 98/1, 103, *111/2*, 119, 120, 122, 125, 130-1, 134, 136, 141, 146, 147, 161, 166/2, 177, 187, 188-9, *190-1*, 192-3, 201; Cambridge University Library: 48; Master and Fellows of Christ Church, Oxford: 22, 50, 62, 67, 84/1, 84/2, 85/1, 85/2, 85/3, 85/4; Giraudon: 92; Guildhall Library: 43/2, 174; Historical Pictures Service, Chicago: 166/1; Michael Holford Picture Library: *36/1*, *36/2*; A. F. Kersting: 207; London Museum: 38/1, 104; National Monuments Record: 47, 53, 72, 214-5; National Portrait Gallery: 192; National Gallery: 210; Phoebus Picture Library: 153, 196; Pitkin Pictorial Ltd: 30, 129, 162/1, 163, 213; Rheinisches Bildarchiv: 153; Royal Scottish Museum: 111/1; Thomas Photos: 158-9, 212/1; Victoria and Albert Museum: 46, 78; Dean and Chapter of Westminster: 54; Dean and Chapter of Winchester: 55, 212/2; Dean and Canons of Windsor: 126/1, 126/2, 127.

Picture research by Jane Dorner.

Numbers in italics refer to colour illustrations.

1
A Treasonable Childhood
1312-27

THE LIFE OF KING EDWARD III was a double tragedy. He inherited an ancient and august throne in circumstances of the greatest dishonour and difficulty. He surmounted these handicaps with skill and courage. Not only did he restore his family's reputation: he made himself into the greatest warrior in Christendom; governed an exacting and acrimonious nation with prudence and tolerance during a period of rapid social change and military peril; enabled this nation to find a new community of spirit, and a sense of political and cultural unity it had never before possessed; and then, when old age had robbed him of his strength and his acumen, saw his achievements vanish, his character soiled and the model commonwealth he had built dissolve into political factions.

England in the early fourteenth century was a consultative monarchy. The English throne, next to the Papacy, was the oldest political institution in western Europe, invested with a unique panoply of traditional ceremonial and dignity. The Crown lands comprised nearly a fifth of England, and its power was buttressed by an efficient central administration, a strong currency and a tax-system which, in theory at least, allowed it to maintain a monopoly of large-scale violence. But the king was required to rule in accordance with ancient law and custom, and with the advice and consent of his prelates and magnates. His freedom of action was further circumscribed by a growing volume of statutory law, which bound himself as well as his subjects. His needs made the raising of emergency revenue essential, from time to time; but this could be done only in a Parliamentary context; and while the Commons were not yet an integral part of Parliament, these assemblies nevertheless represented the nation, and could and did voice its complaints and enforce its demands.

But while the king was not a free agent, he was expected to be a chief executive in every sense of the word: head of government, fountain of justice, commander-in-chief and arbiter of economic policy. There was no means whereby he could constitutionally delegate any of his responsibilities – enforcing the law, balancing the national books, regulating and maintaining the Church or leading his army and his navy in battle. This system imposed imperious, and ultimately intolerable, strains on the monarch. He had to be omni-competent and

Edward III attacks
the Scots.

14

qui deuoient demourer a che

ubiquitous, to travel vast distances on horseback throughout the year and to attend to a multitude of highly technical duties. Always, he had to maintain the *gravitas* of an English sovereign. The Normans and their Plantagenet successors were a race of energetic and capable men. But even the ablest of them wilted under the pressures of the system: and creeping time was the great enemy.

England, by the standards of the high Middle Ages, was an exceptionally prosperous and orderly kingdom. But the geopolitical system of north-west Europe placed it in constant peril; and the Channel was a temptation to disarm as much as a barrier to conquest. The English state was by wealth and population the paramount power in the British Isles. But the final subjection of the Celtic territories of Ireland and Wales, let alone the Norman-Celtic kingdom of Scotland, was beyond its means, and their continued independence a constant threat to its security. In France, the Crown possessed the duchy of Aquitaine, a vital source of its wealth, for the revenue from Bordeaux equalled and sometimes exceeded what the king could extract from the royal estates in England. But Aquitaine was under constant threat from an expanding French monarchy, which had already absorbed England's other cross-Channel possessions, and which increasingly personified the national aims of more than twenty million French-speaking people — a Continental giant many times the size of England in population and resources. France was in intermittent, and often active, alliance with the Scottish Crown; and Irish rebels and Welsh pretenders were maintained at the French Court. Thus England faced the permanent threat of a war of encirclement. Its only apparent remedy was to complete the conquest of the Celtic fringe, and at the same time render the French Crown impotent: aims which, in combination, were beyond its power. English insecurity bred English aggression, and military and financial overcommitment. The problem was insoluble. But it was one which all English kings were called upon to solve. Hence, superimposed upon a political system which made exorbitant demands on the monarch's strength, was a chronic international dilemma which neither diplomacy nor war – nor both in combination – could resolve.

The dilemma darkened the last years of Edward I, the ablest

OPPOSITE Philip IV of France, the father-in-law of Edward II, riding out of a city. In the foreground are scenes showing the persecution of the Templars.

of the Plantagenets. This great law-giver and man of action imposed a military settlement on the Welsh, but failed to extinguish the Scottish monarchy, and in his old age proved unable to stem the steady French encroachments on his Continental possessions. He handed his despised son, Edward II, a dangerous legacy. Edward of Caernarvon seems to us today the most pitiful of English monarchs. He aroused little pity in his own day: it was not a sentiment to which an Englishman born to be king could appeal. His father vested all his hopes in him, and proclaimed him at birth Prince of the new Welsh territory of the Crown. He wanted his son to be like himself: a warrior, a state-lawyer and a tireless administrator. A touching entry in the royal inventory shows that, at the age of six, the Prince was given a toy fortress – probably a model of Caernarvon Castle – carved of brightly-painted wood by one of his father's military architects. But it soon became clear that young Edward had neither the gifts nor the will to emulate his father. He rejected the company and the manners of the older generation of experienced barons and knights who surrounded the King, and chose his friends from a young group of Frenchmen, who had little land or status in England, and who were widely regarded as effeminate, if not sodomitic. Edward I and his son quarrelled violently. The Prince and his friends were expelled from Court, and he was reluctantly allowed to return only on condition that he renounced all ties with his closest confidant, Piers Gaveston. When the old King died, Edward II took office not merely against a background of international crisis but in the public knowledge that he had been judged unworthy by a much-feared and much-respected father.

Ironically, Edward's fatal handicap was his one apparent virtue: his capacity for friendship. If he was nothing else, he was fanatically faithful to those he loved. We cannot now say for certain whether he was homosexual. Only one chronicler, writing fifty years later, refers to it specifically. But his own contemporary biographer writes darkly of the Biblical story of David and Jonathan, and of 'a love which is said to have surpassed the love of women'. It is clear that, in Court and baronial circles, it was generally thought he was a sodomite and, worse, the passive partner. That a king of England should be the 'pathic' of a penniless foreigner like Gaveston (and, later, of the

18

The Life and Times of
EDWARD III

Paul Johnson

Introduction by Antonia Fraser

Weidenfeld and Nicolson
London

0297-76670-8

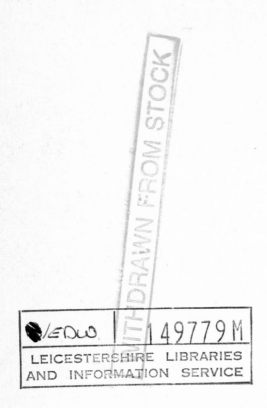
© Weidenfeld and Nicolson
and Book Club Associates 1973

Series design by Paul Watkins
Layout by Juanita Grout

Filmset by Keyspools Ltd, Lancashire
Printed in Great Britain by
Westerham Press Ltd, Westerham, Kent

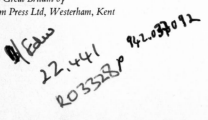

Introduction

Edward iii, that titan whose reign sprawls across fifty years of the fourteenth century – if one could pick one quality which sums up his character in its glorious prime, it would be, in Paul Johnson's striking phrase, his 'huge self-confidence' that he could work with the English nation as a whole. For it is inevitable that in our own age, our interest should focus on such relevant subjects as the growth of English nationalism in the Anglo-French struggle, or more important still, the exact relationship and division of authority between King and Parliament.

Was this not the era of Crécy, that great victory when English longbows of maple, oak and yew, penetrating even the chain-mail of the French kings, made the name of England splendid or at least unforgettable on the Continent? At the end of the day, after fifteen French charges, there were four thousand French knights dead, 'men of superior dignity' said Froissart; they included the King of Bohemia, from whose helmet Edward's son the Black Prince appropriated that famous motto *Ich Dien*. In this reign too the arts flourished harmoniously with the military virtues: it was symbolic that the Court orchestra became a military band in wartime, and what was more, at a slightly higher rate of pay. It was Edward iii who founded the Order of the Garter, in honour of the lovely Joan, Countess of Salisbury, according to a famous story which we are pleased to discover here may even have the ring of truth. English came to replace French as a vernacular language: this was the time of Wycliffe, *Sir Gawayne and the Grene Knight*, and Chaucer's *Canterbury Tales*, which, although written later, evoke that society which Edward iii produced.

Paul Johnson's achievement is to weld this diversity of social development and great events into the coherent story of a reign, and above all the biography of a man. What a magnificent son in his early years was this Edward, born of the pathetic Edward ii, and his Queen Isabella, paramour of Mortimer! But if we concentrate on the King himself, Edward's story must be seen in the end as 'a double tragedy'. The Black Death of 1348 onwards dissolved the society he had known, while the attrition of war made for example, the victory of Poitiers in 1356 less effective than that of Crécy ten years before. So the early domestic achievements too gave way to the degeneration consequent on old age, just as the happy fruitful marriage to Queen Philippa (twelve children ranging from the Black Prince to John of Gaunt) was replaced by the publicly less satisfying relationship with Alice Perrers. A strong-minded woman, who fought for her rights in a man's world, she has probably been unfairly blamed, because her dominance coincided with the weakness of an old man. What is incontrovertible is that the long reign – 1327-77 – ended in military reverses, and those in turn lead to political reverses. Nevertheless that in itself should not detract from the original brightness of this leonine king. It was perhaps inherent in the nature of fourteenth-century monarchy.

Antonia Fraser

Acknowledgments

Photographs and illustrations were supplied by and are reproduced by kind permission of the following: Batsford: 182–3, Bibliothèque Nationale: *2*, *3*, 10, *14-15*, 21, 28, 29, *33*, 42/1, 42/3, 68, 74-5, 88-9, *94-5*, 97, 98, 99, 101, 170-1, 173, *178-9*, 185, 202; Bibliothèque Royale Albert Ier, Brussels: *98*; Bodleian Library: 20/1, 20/2, *45*, 80-1/2, 100, 106, *110*, 116-7, 138-9, 142-3, 155, 156/1, 156/2, 167, 194; British Museum: 13, 17, 25, 34, 35, 38/2, 38/3, 42/2, 43/1, 43/3, 70, 80-1/1, 98/1, 103, *111/2*, 119, 120, 122, 125, 130-1, 134, 136, 141, 146, 147, 161, 166/2, 177, 187, 188-9, *190-1*, 192-3, 201; Cambridge University Library: 48; Master and Fellows of Christ Church, Oxford: 22, 50, 62, 67, 84/1, 84/2, 85/1, 85/2, 85/3, 85/4; Giraudon: 92; Guildhall Library: 43/2, 174; Historical Pictures Service, Chicago: 166/1; Michael Holford Picture Library: *36/1*, *36/2*; A.F.Kersting: 207; London Museum: 38/1, 104; National Monuments Record: 47, 53, 72, 214-5; National Portrait Gallery: 192; National Gallery: 210; Phoebus Picture Library: 153, 196; Pitkin Pictorial Ltd: 30, 129, 162/1, 163, 213; Rheinisches Bildarchiv: 153; Royal Scottish Museum: 111/1; Thomas Photos: 158-9, 212/1; Victoria and Albert Museum: 46, 78; Dean and Chapter of Westminster: 54; Dean and Chapter of Winchester: 55, 212/2; Dean and Canons of Windsor: 126/1, 126/2, 127.

Picture research by Jane Dorner.

Numbers in italics refer to colour illustrations.

1
A Treasonable Childhood
1312-27

THE LIFE OF KING EDWARD III was a double tragedy. He inherited an ancient and august throne in circumstances of the greatest dishonour and difficulty. He surmounted these handicaps with skill and courage. Not only did he restore his family's reputation: he made himself into the greatest warrior in Christendom; governed an exacting and acrimonious nation with prudence and tolerance during a period of rapid social change and military peril; enabled this nation to find a new community of spirit, and a sense of political and cultural unity it had never before possessed; and then, when old age had robbed him of his strength and his acumen, saw his achievements vanish, his character soiled and the model commonwealth he had built dissolve into political factions.

England in the early fourteenth century was a consultative monarchy. The English throne, next to the Papacy, was the oldest political institution in western Europe, invested with a unique panoply of traditional ceremonial and dignity. The Crown lands comprised nearly a fifth of England, and its power was buttressed by an efficient central administration, a strong currency and a tax-system which, in theory at least, allowed it to maintain a monopoly of large-scale violence. But the king was required to rule in accordance with ancient law and custom, and with the advice and consent of his prelates and magnates. His freedom of action was further circumscribed by a growing volume of statutory law, which bound himself as well as his subjects. His needs made the raising of emergency revenue essential, from time to time; but this could be done only in a Parliamentary context; and while the Commons were not yet an integral part of Parliament, these assemblies nevertheless represented the nation, and could and did voice its complaints and enforce its demands.

But while the king was not a free agent, he was expected to be a chief executive in every sense of the word: head of government, fountain of justice, commander-in-chief and arbiter of economic policy. There was no means whereby he could constitutionally delegate any of his responsibilities – enforcing the law, balancing the national books, regulating and maintaining the Church or leading his army and his navy in battle. This system imposed imperious, and ultimately intolerable, strains on the monarch. He had to be omni-competent and

PREVIOUS PAGES Queen Isabella and her army returning from France at the beginning of their expedition to topple Edward II and place his son on the throne.

OPPOSITE God, with his compass, in the midst of the cosmos, from the Holkham Bible picture book of the mid-fourteenth century. With a background of *fleur de lys* recalling Edward's claim to the French throne, this miniature is a compliment to the King, who had inserted a *fleur de lys* on each side of his great seal as early as 1326.

Edward III attacks
the Scots.

14

younger Hugh Despenser) was regarded as intolerable by the baronial establishment. Moreover, what could not be concealed was the King's eccentricities. He was tall, physically strong and fond of exercise – but not of a type sanctioned by custom for a monarch. He had a passion for menial crafts: woodwork and metal-work, thatching, hedging, digging ditches, above all rowing. The last had a symbolic significance, for the ancient paramount kings of England had been rowed in the royal barge by sub-kings as a formal act of submission and servility. For a king to row himself was base, 'unkingly'. The case for Edward's homosexuality seems to be strengthened by the repeated accusation that he consorted on intimate terms with a range of people outside the normal society of a king – according to his biographer, 'singers, actors, grooms, sailors and others of this kind, artists and mechanics'. Equally important, the King had an evident distaste for the normal routine of government, delegating power to a small circle of friends, led by Gaveston, whom he rewarded with manors, castles, offices and titles. The inevitable result was a baronial confederation, calling themselves the Lords Ordainers, who in 1311 forced the King to agree to a charter of provisions, or Ordinances, which bound him to a set of constitutional rules and, in the first place, to the exile of Gaveston and other alien advisers. When Edward broke the Ordinances, the next year, a group of leading barons took to arms, captured Gaveston and executed him without trial.

Five months after this violent affront to the royal dignity, on 13 November 1312, the future Edward III was born at Windsor Castle. His mother, Queen Isabella, daughter of Philip IV of France, was aged sixteen and had married the King four years before: Edward of Windsor was his first-born. The Prince was baptised four days later, being named after his father and grandfather, despite opposition from his French uncle, soon to become Louis X, who wished him to be named after himself. The royal birth was celebrated by a week of festivities in London, the fishmongers constructing and parading a giant model ship, painted with the heraldic blazons of the English and French royal Houses – an unconsciously prophetic act of symbolism. For the King, a healthy heir was some consolation for the loss of Gaveston, and he rapidly invested him with some of Gaveston's confiscated manors and castles, for his maintenance.

19

Edward II was more at
ease with actors, singers
and artists than in the
company of his nobles.
OPPOSITE Masked
mummers from the *Roman
de Fauvel*.
RIGHT A jester from a
psalter of the Bromholm
Priory. (MS Ashmole 1523
f 66)
BELOW Dancers wearing
animal masks.

f auter ne fu gent pour ne denat   e ca chilmali denile
f fon en fonne gvarde mo   pener terfte ftone
A our garde de fear anerine   a m a eft fute pour memorie

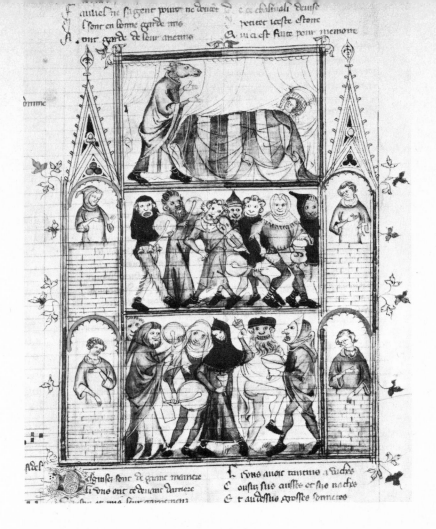

Defgruses fonne de grant mainere   t- rons auoit tantme a fuche
li vno ont redenant farnere   e ouftu fue auffe er fue nache
... ter ma fuer ...   e r au deffus groffe fonneus

Virtually nothing is known of Edward's early years. He was educated by clerks of the royal household, notably Richard of Bury whom he was later (1333) to make Bishop of Durham. Bury was a fine scholar and passionate book-collector, the first great English bibliophile. His treatise on the care of books has survived, and suggests the atmosphere in which Edward was taught to reverence the written word:

> The value of books cannot be expressed. ... Yet a lazy youth will lounge over his book and, in mid-winter, when his nose is oozing mucus, he does not think of wiping it, but allows it to drop on the page before him. If only he had a cobbler's apron in front of him, instead of a book! His nails are black with dirt, with which he marks any passage that strikes him. He sticks in straws to remind him of the bits he had to learn by heart, so that the book becomes so stuffed it tears away from its binding. He eats fruit and cheese over it, and

Edward III with a hawk on his hand. Unlike his father, Edward enjoyed the conventional amusements of the nobility – hawking, hunting and jousting.

drinks wine, all of which leave their traces; and, always chattering, he waters the page with his spittle.

Thanks to Bury, Edward undoubtedly had a good education. Many of his predecessors had been literate too, but his is the first English royal autograph to survive. He was fluent in English and French, knew some German and Flemish, and both spoke and wrote Latin. Contemporary accounts agree that Edward was proficient in all the accomplishments thought suitable for a prince: dancing, singing, hawking, coursing, hunting the red and fallow deer, and handling the sword, lance and cross- and long-bow. He did not inherit his father's low tastes – he was in every respect a conventional member of his

22

class – but he seems throughout his life to have possessed an enviable gift to be affable with men and women of all degrees without the smallest sacrifice of his dignity.

Yet his childhood must have been miserable. The judicial murder of Gaveston opened a period of violent instability in English public life. Gaveston's extinction solved nothing, for the root of the crisis lay in the incapacity and folly of the King himself: the baronial party struck at his favourites because they could not yet steel themselves to the radical course of removing the monarch. They were conservatives, who wished to put the clock back to the good old days of Edward I; events forced them into the role of revolutionaries. They were not only reluctant rebels, but essentially divided ones, for to act against a king was to act also against the hierarchical structure of medieval society, of which they were principal beneficiaries; thus in the complex politics of Edward II's reign it is possible to discern several parties among the magnates, some more radical than others. It was to be Edward III's great merit as a statesman that he was able to persuade the magnates always to act together, of their own volition.

The chief executive task of the monarch was to ensure the defence of the realm; and it was here that Edward II so conspicuously failed. In 1314 the battle of Bannockburn was lost, and northern England exposed to Scottish assault. The immediate result was a Parliament dominated by critics of the King, and the emergence of the Earl of Lancaster, Edward's cousin and the largest landowner in the country, as, in effect, chief minister. But it was not in the nature of English medieval society to permit a dual system of government, with executive power divided among antagonists. Lancaster lacked the necessary magic and authority of kingship, Edward the will to exercise it. He spent the Christmas feast of 1315 in the Cambridge fens, 'rowing with a great concourse of simple people'. In 1319 he organised an ineffectual attempt to retake Berwick, the great northern fortress which was England's 'postern gate' against the Scots; it failed, and Robert the Bruce ravaged as far south as Yorkshire. It was after this failure, says the chronicler Robert of Reading, that Edward's torpor, cowardice and indifference became notorious, and rumours circulated that his lack of capacity must mean he was a bastard. These years were

23

marked by exceptionally heavy rains, floods and ruined harvests, the last period of serious famine England was ever to know. Even the King found it difficult to buy bread for his household in 1316. Price control proved useless: 'How contrary to reason', wrote the chronicler-Canon of Bridlington, 'is an ordinance on prices, when the fruitfulness or sterility of all living things are in the power of God alone.' Distress, accompanied by food riots and near-anarchy, was seen as a divine verdict on the man divinely appointed to rule.

In his weakness, Edward turned increasingly to his private circle, and in particular to Hugh Despenser, the son of one of his father's justiciars, and Despenser's son Hugh. Both were experienced royal officials; the younger had been a member of Edward's household as Prince of Wales, and was reputed to be his lover. Edward had married him to his niece, one of the heiresses to the Gloucester earldom, and he became a great lord in the Welsh Marches. The rise of the Despensers, regarded as 'new men', antagonised not only northern magnates, like Lancaster, but rival Marcher lords, and political crisis drifted into civil war. In 1322, at Boroughbridge, Edward won his one victory, defeating Lancaster's forces and beheading him without trial. Twenty of his supporters were hanged, and Roger Mortimer, chief of the ancient Marcher nobility, sent to the Tower. A docile Parliament repealed the Ordinances, and the estates of the rebels were divided among Edward's supporters, the Despensers taking the lion's share.

The personal rule of the Despensers made inevitable a direct challenge to the King's authority, because they were identified with a personal system of monarchy regarded as unconstitutional. Public funds flowed freely into their pockets: the younger Hugh, by 1324, had deposits of over £6,000 with the Florentine banking houses of Bardi and Peruzzi; and in the next two years he deposited a further £5,735 with the Peruzzi alone. Moreover, they were unsuccessful in handling external affairs. In 1323 they were obliged to sign a humiliating truce with the Scots, and they negotiated ineffectually with the French, who were encroaching in Aquitaine.

It is at this point that Edward of Windsor enters history, as an agent, but seemingly a willing one, of his mother, Queen Isabella. Edward II and his Queen drifted apart only slowly,

OPPOSITE Edward II from *A Chronicle of the Kings of England*.

24

Edwardus kaништан.

of Anno dmi ꝯ᷒ ꝯ᷒ ...
Regnavit apꝝ roꝯ ...
kandeſan in anno ...
ꝯꝯleto ꝯ᷒ꝓ kuland ...
de kepley ccſius ...
Gloudus depoſit᷒ ...
ꝯꝓndada ...
in actū .
cepit ꝯ᷒ magia acc...
duoſ Annoſ ꝯ ...

which suggests that his homosexuality was not as blatant as many supposed. She bore him a second son, John of Eltham, in 1316, a daughter, Eleanor of Woodstock, in 1318, and another, Joan of the Tower, as late as 1321. The break seems to have come after Boroughbridge, and it may be that she was then already attached to Roger Mortimer. When Mortimer escaped from the Tower in 1323, and fled to France, the royal marriage broke up. The next year the Queen's estates were sequestered; and Hugh the Younger made preliminary efforts to secure a papal annulment. Of this, however, there was no question: the English episcopate was already sharply divided on Edward's personal rule. One group, led by Bishop Stapledon of Exeter, were civil servants closely attached to the Court; most of the rest sided with the Queen and her baronial supporters, and Edward's efforts to remove them had already provoked papal wrath. Early in 1325, in an attempt to solve the problem of his spouse, the King was reluctantly persuaded to allow her to leave for France, nominally as a personal envoy to her brother, the French King, in reality as an exile. This was Edward's first mistake; and he compounded it when he allowed his heir, a few months later, to join his mother in France. The young Prince, now thirteen, had just been created Duke of Gascony and Count of Ponthieu, and the purpose of his visit was to do formal homage, on Edward II's behalf, for these territories to Charles IV. Once in Paris, Edward of Windsor became the pawn of Isabella and Mortimer, now living openly together; and Stapledon, who had accompanied him, quickly returned, to warn the King that there was a conspiracy against his throne. Isabella confirmed this by writing a letter to her husband stating flatly that neither she nor her son would return so long as the Despensers were at Court. She planned to invade the country with troops furnished by her brother; but these he declined to supply, giving her relationship with Mortimer as the reason. Instead, she moved to Flanders, and borrowed from William II, Count of Hainault, Holland and Zeeland, some seven hundred men, and ships, in return for betrothing her son to his daughter Philippa.

The young Edward seems to have played a passive role in this treasonable conspiracy, though later tradition has it that he himself selected Philippa (the Count had other daughters). No hint of his personal feelings towards his father or mother survives from the evidence. What does survive, however, is a moving and dignified letter to him from the King, pleading with him to return to his allegiance:

> We command and charge you, on the faith and love you ought to bear us, and on our blessing, that you show yourself our dear and well-beloved son, as you have done before; forget your mother's excuses, and those you have written to us, and come to us here with all haste, that we may ordain for you and your estate as honourably as you may wish. By right and reason, you ought to have no other governor than us, nor should you wish to have. And, dear son, we order you not to marry until you return to us, or without our advice and consent. ...

There is a footnote:

> Edward, fair son, you are very young; take our commandments tenderly to heart; act with humility, and so avoid our reproach, our grief and indignation, and advance your interest and honour. ... For you may be sure that if you now act against our council, and continue in wilful disobedience, you will feel it for the rest of your life, and other sons will take example to disobey their lords and fathers.

If young Edward responded, his reply is lost: perhaps none was sent. Five months later, he sailed with his mother's expedition from Dordrecht (September 1326), landing the next day at Orwell in Suffolk. The King had tried to raise a fleet, but the sailors refused to put out, 'because of the great anger they had towards Sir Hugh Despenser'. He failed, also, to defend London; indeed the mob rose against him, dragged Bishop Stapledon from his horse, executed him with a butcher's knife, and sent the head to the Queen. The King retreated west, closely followed by the growing forces of Isabella; at Oxford she heard Bishop Orleton, one of her supporters, preach to the text 'I will put enmity between thee and the woman, and between her seed and thy seed.' Bristol was yielded by the elder Despenser, who was promptly judged guilty of treason by the magnates, 'his guilt being notorious' – thus embodying the ancient concept of manifest ill-fame, which made trial and evidence superfluous. He was hanged. His son and the King fled to Wales, where they were hunted down and captured by

Queen Isabella and her forces are welcomed by the people of Bristol.

Henry of Leicester, brother and heir of the executed Earl of Lancaster. Some royal clerks were drawn and quartered. Young Despenser was brought before a so-called 'tribunal', presided over by a justice from the Lancaster estates, William Trussell, and ordered to be hanged, drawn and quartered, judgment being given by *'totes les bones gentz du Roialme, greindres et meindres, riches et poures, par commun assent'* ('all the good people of the Kingdom, great and lesser, rich and poor, by common assent').

Revenge against the Despenser faction had been swift and sweet. But what to do with their master, the King? By the end of October, his son had been proclaimed by the magnates Keeper of the Realm, and had begun to issue writs for a Parliament, in his father's name, but under his own privy seal. There was no constitutional machinery to depose and replace a king; thus, on top of a series of judicial murders, the magnates

28

The quartering of Hugh
Despenser the Younger.

had to proceed by legal fiction. Uncomfortable in their revolutionary role, wishing to spread the responsibility as widely as possible, and to preserve the apparatus of legality, they summoned a huge Parliament which crowded into Westminster Hall. All present – bishops, abbots, priests, clerks, earls, barons, judges, knights, barons of the Cinq Ports and burgesses – proceeded to the Guildhall and swore a confederate oath; the swearings took three days. On 15 January 1327, the Archbishop of Canterbury preached to the text 'vox populi, vox dei', and announced that all estates had decided that Edward III should succeed; Articles of Deposition were read out, charging his father with incompetence, failure to take wise counsel, destroying the Church, losing Scotland, Ireland and Gascony, breaking his coronation oath to do justice, and being of incorrigible cruelty and weakness. A deputation under Trussell, described as 'Procurator of the Realm', was sent to Kenilworth, where

Edward II was held, and told the King, who was in tears and wearing a black gown, that if he abdicated he would be maintained in dignity; if not, Parliament would appoint a king from outside the royal blood. Edward consented, and the next day his steward broke his staff of office and dissolved the royal household, the new reign dating from 25 January. Two days before he was crowned, Edward III, aged fourteen, issued a proclamation falsely stating that his father had taken the decision 'of his own good will and by common consent of the prelates, earls, barons and other nobles, and the community of the realm'. Edward III was the first king of England to rule by a Parliamentary title.

A deposed monarch was virtually a dead man. Mortimer had him moved to Berkeley Castle, whose grim silhouette still rises like a phantom from the mists of the Severn water-meadows. Its owner was Thomas, Lord Berkeley, a Mortimer client by marriage, and a bitter victim of the old King's injustices: not a charitable gaoler. His official keepers were Sir John Maltravers and Sir Thomas Gurney. Hardly any prelates or magnates had stood by Edward II, and only two officials; nevertheless, rescue attempts were made, one coming near to success. As a result, Edward was thrown into a castle pit, the repository of the carcasses of diseased cattle, in the hope that he would die of asphyxiation; but his body was strong, and he survived, covered in filth and matted hair. In September 1327, Mortimer sent an envoy, William Ogle, to Berkeley with verbal instructions; a fortnight later it was announced that Edward II had died of natural causes. There were no marks on the body. The most likely explanation of Edward's death is provided by John Trevisa, in his English translation, with interpolations, of Higden's *Polychronicon*. Trevisa, who was born in the little town of Berkeley, was a child at the time, and later served Lord Thomas as chaplain. He must have known the truth, and he states that Edward was killed 'with a hoote broche putte thro the secret place posterialle'. The body was taken to Gloucester Abbey and buried with considerable state, in the unctuous presence of Isabella. The young King was also there, but his feelings are unknown, and now unknowable.

We must assume that Edward III, who shared to the full the prevailing wisdom, the likes and dislikes, prejudices and

OPPOSITE The magnificent tomb in Gloucester Cathedral erected by Edward III for his father, whose memory won the reverence that he had never known in his lifetime. Within a few years pilgrims were flocking to view the alabaster effigy, which depicts him in a pose of serene majesty.

31

antipathies of his class and society – who was in fact a well-adjusted extrovert, perfectly suited to his role in life – was ashamed of his father. Such filial piety as he had, he expressed in form rather than substance. In due course, he built over the body a splendid tomb: an alabaster effigy of his father, whose sweeping curves are the outstanding example of what might be termed English fourteenth-century baroque, surmounted by a gossamer canopy of stone. The tomb became a shrine, 'so that within a few years there was such a concourse of people that the city of Gloucester could scarcely house the multitude'; and 'the offerings of the faithful who flocked to the king's tomb' were so great that the Abbot was able to rebuild the choir in the new Perpendicular style, the first architectural expression of English nationalism. Edward III made a half-hearted attempt to promote the cult of his father as a national king-saint, to rival St Louis of France, but soon settled for the already venerable (but equally undistinguished) Edward the Confessor; it was left to his grandson, Richard II, actively to promote Edward II's canonisation, though with no success. Three hundred years later, the poet Thomas Gray wrote his epitaph:

> Weave the warp and weave the woof,
> The winding sheet of Edward's race;
> Give ample room and verge enough,
> The characters of Hell to trace.
> Mark the year and mark the night,
> When Severn shall reecho with the fright,
> The shrieks of death through Berkeley's roof that ring,
> Shrieks of an agonising king.

In 1330 Edward III instituted perfunctory proceedings against his father's murderers. Thomas Berkeley successfully established his legal innocence; the other three were judged guilty and fled. Nothing more is heard of Ogle; Gurney died abroad; Maltravers had his sentence reversed, his estates restored, and died in 1364, an honoured knight of Parliament. Perhaps rightly, Edward decided that these men were mere agents and that, if revenge were appropriate, it must fall on Mortimer.

OPPOSITE The coronation of Edward III at the age of fourteen.

e couronnement du roy
eduart dingleterre. Le
xviiie. Chapitre.

Pres que les pl̃s
des compaignons
de haynault se
furent partiz

2 The Dishonoured

Inheritance 1327-30

LEFT A fourteenth-century French panel showing a soul rescued from the mouth of hell.
BELOW The Fall of Babylon from the Apocalypse tapestry made by Jean Blondel *c.* 1377 for Louis I of Anjou.

Edward III became king by means which were, perhaps, inevitable in the circumstances, but which reflected shame on himself, and cast doubt on his authority and on the repute of the Crown itself. Moreover, he was still a minor, though an increasingly aware, articulate and angry one. Nominally, there was a Regency Council, presided over by Henry of Leicester, now made Earl of Lancaster. The sentence on his brother was reversed, and his estates restored. But Mortimer himself did not serve on the Council, presumably because he did not choose to subordinate himself to Lancaster; and was represented instead by two of his mistress's episcopal creatures, Hotham of Ely, the Chancellor, and Orleton of Hereford, the Treasurer. But there is no doubt that he possessed a real measure of power, and in particular power over the King's person. Indeed, the fatal dualism of Edward II's reign reappeared: on the one hand, the shadow of authority resting in the constitutional machinery approved by Parliament; and, on the other, its substance exercised by a Court faction, and an increasingly rapacious one. The situation could not be expected to endure; the only question was, when and how the dichotomy would be ended, and what part the young King would play in resolving it.

We must always be careful in believing medieval chroniclers when they accuse those exercising power of personal greed; often, those recording events could not, or would not, distinguish between the legitimate business of raising royal revenue and the private pursuit of wealth. But even making allowances for this, Isabella and Mortimer seem to have exploited their position with a ruthlessness even the Despensers might have admired. The Queen-Mother got her dower increased to the enormous annual sum of 20,000 marks (£13,333), and appropriated the movables (including cash), plate and jewels of young Despenser. Her eye alighted on small, as well as large, trophies: it was a particular grievance of clerical scribes that she confiscated books on Canon Law, worth £10, presented by her husband to the Master of King's Hall, Cambridge. Mortimer concentrated his attention on enlarging his base in Wales, where political and military power could become the key to the kingdom. He got back his own property, plus an enormous block of confiscated land in Wales and the Marches; this, together with his appointment as Justiciar of Wales, gave

PREVIOUS PAGES Edward III depicted on the front and back of his great seal.

37

Precious objects of the
fourteenth century, such as
were beloved by Queen
Isabella.
ABOVE RIGHT A French
silver-gilt bowl;
RIGHT Enamelled
candlesticks;
ABOVE A pitcher with
applied decoration.

him control of what was, in effect, a sovereign kingdom. In 1328 he was made Earl of March, a title, says one chronicler angrily, never before bestowed on a subject. He was in direct descent of the Mortimers established in Wales by the Conqueror; and he claimed, moreover, a mythical descent from Arthur and the supposed first king of Britain, Brutus. On this basis, he held a Round Table tournament at Bedford, and entertained the King and the Court in style at his border strongholds.

But if Mortimer and the Queen-Mother could seize the spoils of office, they were manifestly unable to unify and galvanise the nation into the kind of forceful activity which the international situation required. When the border truce with the Scots broke down, as was inevitable, the English were forced to retire into Newcastle, and there was no alternative but to make peace, on Scots terms. The young King felt humiliated and said so – his first indication of an independent spirit; he signed the Treaty of Northampton (1328) with reluctance. The treaty conceded Bruce all he had fought for, recognised him as sovereign of an independent kingdom and provided for a marriage between Edward's young sister, Joan, and Bruce's four-year-old son, David. What is more, the English agreed to surrender the documentary evidence of individual acts of homage by the Scots nobility, known as the Ragman Roll, and the captured Stone of Scone – the visible trophies of Edward I's heroic efforts. It was, said one chronicler, a *turpis pax* ('a shameful peace') – and a worthless one, too, for its terms could not be enforced. The Abbot of Westminster, backed by the London mob, refused to hand over the Stone; and the Ragman Roll remained in the Tower archives. As the English had not complied with the treaty, there was nothing to prevent Bruce resuming his attacks. And, as a final insult, much of the £20,000 provided by the Scots as compensation for their destruction of property in the north was in fact seized by Isabella.

More significant, in the long run, was Mortimer's handling of relations with France. And at this point we must examine in a little detail the legal, and the concrete, issues raised by Edward's position as a duke and a count of France. The anomaly of a sovereign of one state holding land as a feudatory of another was not unique or new; in England's case it went back to the Conquest. But it had always raised difficulties, which centuries of fighting and diplomacy had failed to resolve. No one disputed the title of the Plantagenets to the duchy of Aquitaine, which had descended to them through the great Eleanor, wife of Henry II. What was at issue was the manner in which it was held. Was it, as the English maintained, an *alod*, held in full sovereignty? Or was it, as the French argued, a simple tenancy-in-chief, making the King-Duke a peer of France, bound to swear full allegiance to the French king, to come to his aid against his enemies and to submit his judgments to appeals in the French king's Court? The Treaty of Paris, which Henry III had signed in 1259, appeared to concede the French case, but it was hedged with qualifications, and its terms, and their interpretations, had been glossed by a mountain of juristic learning. Three expert clerks had been employed for years by poor Bishop Stapledon, compiling vast calendars of Gascon documents, themselves housed in mildewed cartulary racks and chests. The dispute was the *Jarndyce v. Jarndyce* of the Middle Ages, with no prospect of a final settlement being reached in the courts.

Neither side, it is true, was anxious in theory to press its case to extremes, which meant the incalculable verdict of war. In 1303, the ageing Edward I sought to postpone a decision by marrying his son to the daughter of the French king; thus, Edward II was son-in-law to Philip IV, and brother-in-law to his three successors. But the intermarriage of potential royal enemies raised as many problems as it solved. In February 1328 the last of Philip's sons died childless. If women were barred from the French throne, as the Salic Law theoretically supposed, his heir was Philip of Valois, Charles IV's nephew. If not, the best claim lay with the son of Philip IV's daughter, his direct descendant Edward III.

Beneath these legalistic and theoretical issues lay the realities of the situation on the ground, among the towns and villages and fields of south-west France, for the dispute over Aquitaine and Ponthieu revolved not merely around the nature of the King-Duke's homage, but in the physical frontiers of these territories, which had always been doubtful, and which were constantly changing by death, inheritance, sub-division and sale. The only sure claim was one enforcible by control on the spot: and this meant actual possession of fortified strongpoints, directly administered by the rival Crowns. They were called *bastides*, or town-colonies, and both sides had been planting them for over a century. Edward I had built many *bastides* in Gascony, as he had in Wales, southern Scotland and parts of England: they were the only guarantee that his writs would run in the countryside they covered. But the money to surround them with fortified walls had rarely been available; and, without defences, they were hostages to fortune, and the certain objects of dispute. Moreover, the French Crown also had been building *bastides* in the disputed territories, in greater numbers and with more ample resources. By the 1320s the proximity of rival centres of power brought the respective jurisdictions into conflict, with appeals to the French Crown. If the English king accepted the ultimate competence of the French courts, the verdicts would go against him; if he rejected it, he was in contempt, and the punishment was forfeiture of his duchy. This was the ultimate French deterrent. The ultimate English deterrent was to lay claim to the French crown itself. Neither side wished to use these weapons. Both eventually felt compelled to do so. The result was what is called the Hundred Years' War.

But in the 1320s, with a succession of weak governments in England, Edward's case went by default. In 1328, Isabella told a French embassy that her son, the son of a king, could never do homage to the son of a count (Philip of Valois). Edward's claim was explicitly reserved. But in the meantime, Philip VI was crowned king at Rheims, and Edward III travelled over to France to do him homage the following year. The homage was simple, which begged any number of questions, and hedged with reservations. Nevertheless, the reality was that the Valois claimant had established himself, against a background of English military impotence, and that English control of the duchy of Aquitaine had been reduced to a narrow coastal strip. Most of the charges which Isabella and Mortimer had levelled against the king they had murdered could be made, with equal justice, against themselves.

By early 1330 the Isabella-Mortimer faction, though still powerful in physical terms, was constitutionally and morally isolated. Mortimer now committed an act of folly against an

The French Succession

The question of the French succession contributed to the Hundred Years' War. Philip IV, shown on the right with his family, was succeeded in turn by his three sons: Louis X (below left), Philip V (below right), and Charles IV; but all died without sons to succeed them.

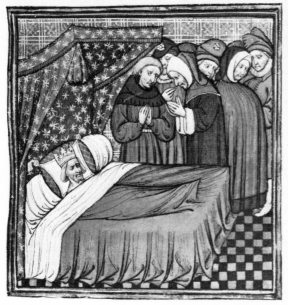

On the death of Charles
IV (above left) the French
nobility met to discuss the
succession (above right). If
women were barred from
the throne by Salic Law,
the heir was Philip of
Valois, nephew to Charles
IV. If not, Edward III
could claim the throne as
the son of Philip's
daughter, Isabel.

The French crowned
Philip of Valois as Philip VI
in 1328 (right) but Edward
reserved his claim and used
it as a pretext of war and a
weapon of negotiation in
the years ahead.

imprudent but respected member of the establishment, Edward II's younger half-brother, the Earl of Kent. He was induced by *agents-provocateurs* to engage in a plot to restore his brother, whom he was persuaded was still living; and then detected, seized, tried and executed. This almost pointless crime seems to have been the catalyst in placing Edward III at the head of the opposition against his nominal rule. Indeed, he had little alternative, for the logic of Mortimer's actions was to seize the crown for himself; with every month that passed, Edward became fitter for the actual discharge of his royal duties. At a Parliament summoned at Nottingham in October 1330, we have a vivid description, by the chronicler Geoffrey le Baker, of Mortimer's behaviour: 'A greater acclamation was given him than that of the king. ... He let the King stand in his presence, and used to walk arrogantly beside the new King, never letting the King go before him, but sometimes going in front himself.' A rumour, says Baker, swept through the town that Mortimer 'thirsted for the destruction of the royal blood and the usurpation of the royal majesty'. It was plain that Mortimer could not remain in this equipoise; he must go forward, and destroy the last Plantagenet, or risk certain destruction himself.

Instead, Edward carried out a pre-emptive strike, with the connivance of Lancaster, and with the active assistance of two members of his household – his tutor, Bury, Keeper of the Privy Seal, and one of his yeomen, William Montague. The latter travelled secretly to the Pope, to secure his acquiescence, and on his return Bury sent the Pope a letter, enclosing a holograph specimen of Edward's and a code-signal, *'pater sancte'*, to indicate which future communications came from the King himself, as opposed to letters drafted by Isabella and her lover. In the event, these precautions were unnecessary. Edward was now fast emerging as an adult, and a confident man of action. With Montague, he got access to Nottingham Castle by a secret passage, and simply arrested Mortimer, in person, in his bedchamber. The walls of Jericho, such as they were, fell without even the need for a trumpet-blast. Mortimer's two night-guards were killed in a brief struggle, and Isabella, who was present, evidently feared that her lover was to be executed on the spot. But Edward was too shrewd for that. The next morning he issued a proclamation stating that he was taking the

OPPOSITE Edward III receives a sword and shield from St George. St George epitomised the virtues of honour, courage, and chivalry which Edward was to make fashionable in his court. He was chosen as the patron saint of the Order of the Garter.

A bronze figure of virtue
triumphing over vice,
c. 1330.

OPPOSITE Castle Rising in
Norfolk, where Queen
Isabella was sent to end her
days in virtuous
retirement.

government into his own hands, and he promptly sent out
writs summoning a new Parliament in Westminster, commanding the sheriffs to ensure that the knights of the shire to be
elected were 'proper and sufficient' men, willing and able to
bring forward the grievances of their districts and advise on
their redress. It may be said that Edward, once he had seized the
reins of power, until the moment when darkness and debility
closed in upon him, always exhibited a huge self-confidence in
his ability to work with the nation as a whole, even when he
was under criticism. His Parliaments were as representative as
he could make them, and from this time the Commons were
always part of them.

Mortimer was taken to the Tower, and when Parliament met
was charged before his peers with usurping royal power,
murdering King Edward II, appearing with force at the
Parliament, encompassing the death of the Earl of Kent,
illegally obtaining from the Crown numerous castles and other
property, and appropriating the King's treasure and the Scottish
compensation. Geoffrey le Baker noted: 'He was condemned
to death by his peers, but he did not appear before them nor
was he allowed to make any defence, since from the deaths of
the earls of Lancaster, Winchester, Gloucester and Kent nobles
were not allowed to defend themselves, but perished without
defence and lawful conviction.' His 'notoriety' was judged to
be sufficient proof and 'he was drawn and hanged on the
common gallows of thieves at the Elms' (Tyburn).

Thus, though Mortimer in turn was judicially murdered, this
was in fact to be the last in the long series of vendettas at the
summit of English society which had undermined the due
process of law since the death of Edward I. Only two of
Mortimer's associates followed him to the gallows. Edward
was no doubt impressed by the fact that none of Mortimer's vast
Welsh and Marcher territories had stirred on his behalf, and that
revenge was needless and impolitic. In particular, he took no
legal action against his mother, who was virtually excluded
from the bill of charges against Mortimer. For this, he had
several additional reasons: affection, perhaps; more likely an
unwillingness to inflict further damage on the image of royalty,
which had been so woefully besmirched in the last twenty years;
also, a prescient appreciation of the fact that his claims to the

46

Si non essent registrantes et futuris ministrantes que vident et que audiunt. et illa que euemunt in diuersis temporibus et in suis etatibus p̃ libros et per scripturas vbi po̅uit magnas curas. pauca sc̃ rentur de factis in temporibus transactis. Idarco sunt comme̅ dandi et q̅ plurimum laudan di qui faciunt registrare nota bilia. et quare? quia sepe legen tibus et studere uolentibus da̅t solamen et gaudium. quia per bonum studium legunt, videt. meditantur. et super visis le cantur quando noua reperiunt

que non viderunt nec sciunt. per scripturas eto cemur si nos bene recordemur. que sunt bona vt amemur. quid ue malu̅ vt iutemur. Ergo tu sc̃ie co̅ clude ama scripturas. et stude. et non amabis vicia. In quib̅ sunt opprobria. Laudandum est multum scire scripturas et sic finire. Nam sunt scientie pl̃ res. de luctatibus non aures. C̅ parum profiunt. et animar̅ iusiciunt. Si studes in primi tuis ato eris sciens si vis. Est quoq̅ philosophia lauda bilis sciencia. Nam sc̃ientes laudantur. et a cunctis hono

French crown came through his mother, who must therefore be accorded the respect due to her lineage. At all events, he merely reduced her dower to £3,000, and settled her at Castle Rising in Norfolk, where she bullied the burghers of King's Lynn. It is not true, as has often been stated, that she was a virtual prisoner. On the contrary, though Edward visited her annually at Rising, she was free to move about, and on at least one occasion (in 1344), she attended a great feast at Windsor Castle, where she was accorded her place as Queen-Mother. She spent her time hawking, reading and collecting relics; and in her old age she took the habit of the Poor Clares, and was buried in the Franciscan church at Newgate in 1358. Edward's handling of the loose ends left by the Mortimer episode shows a nice sense of diplomacy, which went some way to restoring the reputation of his parents, without digging up inconvenient old bones.

OPPOSITE The burial of plague victims near Tournai in 1339.

3
Learning to be King
1330-41

DURING THE FIRST DECADE of his personal rule, Edward was learning to be king. He moved with decision and confidence, on a variety of fronts, and exhibited considerable skill. But he made mistakes, too, some of them serious. It was his ability to learn from his errors, and to retreat quickly from untenable positions, which marks him as a notable civil statesman. Indeed, it can be argued that he profited more from his political misjudgments than from his military ones. One salient principle runs through his reign: the quest for national reconciliation and unity, the attempt to realise the medieval image of the community as an organism, a body, each of whose parts worked in conjunction with the others in its predestined role. This policy was made imperative by recent events, which had threatened the basic stability of the kingdom: it was also dictated by the need to prepare and solidify the nation against the great series of wars which men felt were coming.

It is in his handling of the great men of the realm that we see Edward at his best, following very much in the pattern of his grandfather. These were the men the King had to work with; the fewer enemies among them, the more friends, the better; hence his prompt refusal to persecute the Mortimer faction. Indeed, Edward was not merely forgiving; he was generous. Mortimer's followers were even advanced. Orleton was given an embassy to France, and shortly promoted to Winchester, richest of the English sees. Bishop Burghersh was back in office as Treasurer by 1334. His mother's friends Wyville and Hotham kept their sees, and Bishop Airmyn of Norwich was brought into the government. One of Mortimer's men, Sir Oliver Ingham, was restored to his key post as Seneschal of Aquitaine; Burghersh's nephew, Bartholemew, became a close friend of Edward, and later master of his son's household. Nor did Edward reconcile his enemies at the expense of his friends. The small group who backed his *coup* in 1330 were rapidly advanced. Montague gained much of the Mortimer lands, a peerage in 1331 and an earldom (of Salisbury) six years later; his brother became a bishop. Bury was made Chancellor in 1334 and Bishop of Durham. William Clinton, another agent in the *coup*, became Warden of the Cinq Ports and Earl of Huntingdon, and a fourth, Robert Ufford, Steward of the Household and Earl of Suffolk. The older nobility – the Fitzalans, the

PREVIOUS PAGES Edward III enthroned, with knights on the left who represent military service, and tributes being presented on the right. In return for this allegiance the king was expected to be head of government, to enforce the law, to maintain the church and the economy, and to protect his realm by armed might.

52

A corbel head of Edward III from Tewkesbury Abbey.

Beauchamps, the Bohuns, the Audleys – had their lands restored, offices bestowed or were raised to earldoms. The Lancastrian faction, in particular, was brought into the magic circle: Lancaster's heir, Henry of Grosmont, was made Earl of Derby, his clients, the Stratfords, got three bishoprics, including Canterbury and London, and his legal adviser, Trussell, received the lucrative financial post of escheator south of Trent. All these men served Edward faithfully and, with one brief exception, in concord. Most of them fought alongside him in Scotland and in France; Edward was always able to entrust them, in full confidence, with the leading commands. There is no hint of disagreements with the magnates, or of factions within them, until Edward's own grip on events slackened. He led a united nobility, something denied any other sovereign of his day, and this did not come about by chance.

Edward's quest for national unity was enormously aided by his shrewd and likeable queen, Philippa, who bore him his first child, Edward of Woodstock, in June 1330. It is a curious fact that her image and personality stand out far more clearly from the records than her husband's. The chroniclers give us cliché-portraits of the King, as a paragon of knightly virtues – brave,

53

open-handed, forgiving, handsome: 'he had a face like a god', says one, which does not help us much. We gather that his chief characteristic was his affability (clouded, from time to time, by brief spasms of Plantagenet rage), his overriding desire to like and be liked, to avoid scenes and arguments; to jolly along men of all classes: 'He did not like to be sad', says Froissart. Philippa we can see more clearly. As a child, she was described in detail by Stapledon, who looked her over, on Edward II's behalf, as a possible bride for his heir:

> Her hair is nice, between blue-black and brown. Her head is clean-shaped, forehead high and broad. … Her face narrows between the eyes, the lower part more slender than her forehead. Her eyes black-brown and deep, nose smooth and even, broad at the tip and flattened, but not snub; nostrils broad; mouth wide, lips full, especially the lower lip. … Her lower teeth project a little beyond the upper, but this is not much seen. … Nought is amiss so far as a man can see.

Two representations of Queen Philippa: OPPOSITE As the Virgin with her child; BELOW As a serene matron on her tomb at Westminster.

This description accords reasonably well with the various representations of her which have come down to us, even with her funeral effigy in Westminster Abbey, a splendid but truthful work, which ruthlessly portrays her as an ample Flemish matron in late middle age, worn with childbearing but serene and

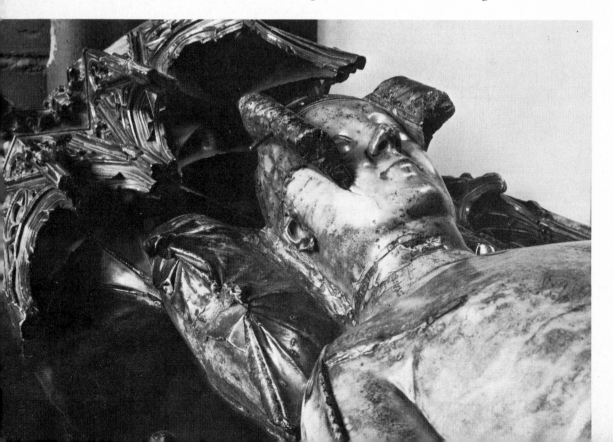

content. Tradition says she suckled her first-born, the future Black Prince, herself (though the documents show that he had a nursemaid), and a statue at Winchester represents her as a virgin, with the babe at her breast. She appears briefly in the chronicles as a conciliator and appeaser, tender and merciful. To her must go much of the credit for the remarkable fact that Edward always remained on excellent terms with his numerous children, something rare in Plantagenet (indeed in English royal) history.

Philippa's fault was her extravagance. Her household was old-fashioned in its structure, offered little opportunities for advancement and thus did not attract able men in the administrative posts. She was constantly in debt, and in 1363 Edward was obliged to amalgamate the households to restore some sort of order. Her taste in dress was gaudy, and Edward indulged it. In 1348, for her 'up-rising' after the birth of her fourth son, he gave her a robe and tunic of blue velvet, worked with gold birds surrounded by large pearls, the ground being powdered with small pearls – four hundred large pearls and thirty-eight ounces of small pearls in all. At the same time, six hundred large pearls and sixteen pounds of gold leaf were used to redecorate her chamber; she was given a new bed, a state cradle and 'a common cradle' for her child, new silver cups, saucers and spoons, and twelve carpets worth £60 (the Black Prince capped this by sending her a new hunter, called 'Banzan de Burgh'). Ten years later, we find the King giving her the huge sum of £500 'for the preparation of her apparel against the feast of St George, to be celebrated at Windsor'. Philippa was a very active woman, and her debts arose, at least in part, from expenses incurred while accompanying Edward on his Continental expeditions – often in great discomfort, sometimes in real danger. She was in every sense a consort.

On the basis of his successful efforts to re-establish national unity, Edward was able to turn to the pressing problems of foreign affairs, and in the first place to the 'postern gate'. Bruce had died in 1329, and his heir was a minor – but also Edward's brother-in-law. Edward might seek to re-establish the English paramountcy through this family alliance; or he might support the pretender to the throne, Edward Balliol, who was willing to acknowledge English suzerainty; but in any event he had to assert English military predominance, and clear the north of Scots. During the next few years, Edward threw his weight behind both factions alternately, while steadily building up his forces. But he could find no political solution to the Scottish problem: the pro-English and the nationalist forces there were too evenly balanced for either to predominate for long, and a final solution for Scotland was to baffle generations of English statesmen until the beginning of the seventeenth century, when James I and VI brought the two kingdoms together. However, what Edward could do, and did do, was to slam the postern-gate shut, and carry the area of warfare north of the border.

In 1332 he moved his government to York, which for the next five years became the administrative capital of England. Large forces were raised and trained under his personal super-vision, and at the end of the year he invested Berwick. The Scots had held the military initiative in recent years by their ability to travel light and fast, and avoid battle except on ground of their own choosing. Now Edward set about the siege in great strength and in a highly professional manner. The Scots felt obliged to send a relieving force, which was as Edward wished. Throughout his military career, his strategy was to force his opponents to give open battle, and his tactics to fight such battles in a defensive posture, in carefully-chosen terrain, with dis-mounted men-at-arms protecting, or flanked by, rapid-firing longbowmen. Edward, briefly, understood the salient principle of warfare – the need to concentrate overwhelming firepower, and then to draw the enemy within its arc. At Halidon Hill, on 13 July 1333, he exercised these methods with complete success, the capitulation of Berwick followed, and for the first time in twenty years, England was cleared of invaders. These victories were important for the King's personal confidence, for his domestic prestige and for his international reputation: for the first time, Europe became aware that a new sun had risen.

But the defeat of the Scots activated the offensive-defensive mechanism of the Franco-Scots alliance. The young Scots King, and the Scots bishops, fled to France, and the French government, with Gascony on its mind, increasingly obtruded Scotland into the already complex problem of Anglo-French disputes. In turn, Edward felt a growing need to switch his attention south. He campaigned in Scotland for the next two years. If a final military solution eluded him, as it had his grandfather, at least the Scottish problem was contained, and it became possible to tackle the much more serious menace of French expansion.

The acute phase of the Anglo-French struggle which we call the Hundred Years' War was not inevitable; but on the other hand, it is hard to see how either party, granted their premises, could have avoided it. Certainly, both tried hard to negotiate a settlement. Recent research shows that Edward recruited to his Chancery a group of highly-trained, experienced and multi-lingual diplomats, and that they were hard at work throughout the 1330s, in intensive correspondence with the various courts involved. In the first third of the century, three protracted sets of negotiations were undertaken with the French. But, and this is significant, they were referred to by the French as 'processes' – that is, in the French view, they constituted a case being heard within the framework of the French legal system, with the French king's Court as the ultimate arbiter. To the English, by contrast, they were negotiations between inde-pendent sovereigns. There could be no reconciliation between these two viewpoints, which indeed enshrined the nub of the problem. The French had the force of history on their side, and English example: no English king could conceivably have tolerated a sovereign enclave on his territory – England was already a unitary state, and France was merely struggling to emulate her.

On the other hand, inconclusive negotiations favoured the French, and allowed the erosion of English Aquitaine to continue. For the English to use the instrument of war was thus a defensive action in this sense, and not only in this sense. France was already a great power, with real, if ill-defined, ambitions. A century before, Philip Augustus had claimed the English crown with the support of the Church (as, in 1066, William of Normandy had actually seized it, at the head of a French coalition); and France now effectively controlled the Papacy. In 1334 Philip VI played the Scotch card, by insisting that a Scottish solution must be included in any Anglo-French treaty, thus arousing the English psychosis of encirclement. Nor was this fear without practical foundation. The prosperity of

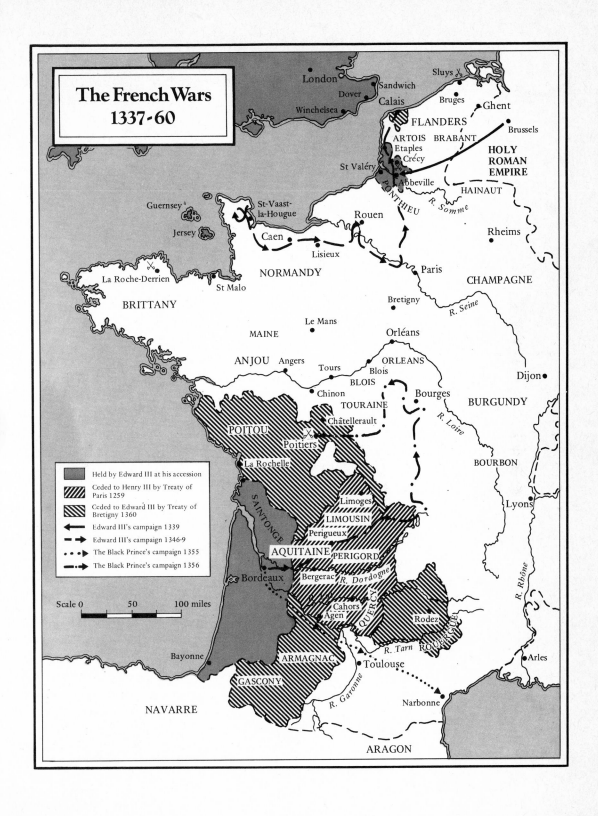

The French Wars 1337-60

London
Sandwich
Dover
Winchelsea
Calais
Sluys
Bruges
Ghent
Brussels

FLANDERS
ARTOIS   BRABANT
Etaples
Crécy
St Valéry
Abbeville
PONTHIEU
HOLY
ROMAN
EMPIRE
HAINAUT
R. Somme

Guernsey
St-Vaast-
la-Hougue
Rouen
Rheims

Jersey
Caen
Lisieux
Paris
CHAMPAGNE

La Roche-Derrien
St Malo
NORMANDY
Bretigny
R. Seine

BRITTANY
Le Mans
Orléans

MAINE
ANJOU   Angers
Tours
ORLEANS
Dijon

Chinon
Blois
BLOIS
Bourges
BURGUNDY

POITOU
TOURAINE
Châtellerault

Poitiers
BOURBON

La Rochelle
Lyons

SAINTONGE
Limoges
LIMOUSIN
Perigueux

AQUITAINE
PERIGORD

Bordeaux
Bergerac   R. Dordogne
QUERCY
R. Rhône

Cahors
Agen
Rodez
ROUERGUE

Bayonne
ARMAGNAC
R. Tarn
Arles

GASCONY
Toulouse

NAVARRE
R. Garonne
Narbonne

ARAGON

Held by Edward III at his accession

Ceded to Henry III by Treaty of
Paris 1259

Ceded to Edward III by Treaty of
Bretigny 1360

Edward III's campaign 1339

Edward III's campaign 1346-9

The Black Prince's campaign 1355

The Black Prince's campaign 1356

Scale 0   50   100 miles

England, and the stability of the Crown itself, depended upon keeping open the sea-lanes – for English wool exports to Flanders, for English wool, grain and salted fish to Bordeaux, for wine imported from Bordeaux and salt from Brittany and Poitou. This trade was heavily taxed, in one way or another: the English state drew more than half its revenues from it. France was becoming a considerable naval power: at Rouen, Philip the Fair had built a modern naval base, unique in north-west Europe, and pointed at the English coast and sea-lanes – where else? France was, too, a regular employer of Genoese and Castilian naval galleys – an expensive commitment, not designed for mere display. The chroniclers picture the war as, to us, a meaningless exercise in chivalry. Fragments of English council minutes, and French archives – notably the papers of Marshal Mile de Noyers – show that more serious issues were involved. In the late 1330s, the French were planning to concentrate a fleet of their own and Genoese galleys at Rouen, with the object of destroying the English merchant fleet and establishing a naval blockade. They intended to attack the English salt, wine, wool and fishing fleets, and these schemes were drawn up in detail, and costed, and their effects on the English Exchequer calculated. The full extent of France's aggressive plans was not known to the English until secret documents fell into their hands after the Battle of Crécy. But they were well aware of the drift. The real signal for war came in 1336, when the French moved their fleet – ostensibly assembled for a crusade – from its base in Marseilles into the English Channel. Thereafter, the French confiscation of Gascony the next year, and Edward's riposte by assuming the royal arms of France, though more than mere formalities, made official a state of war which already existed.

Edward was fully aware of the magnitude of the task before him, and prepared for action with a careful combination of diplomatic and administrative moves. France was a giant, but in some ways a weak giant, involved in a complex series of jurisdictional disputes on her northern and eastern frontiers which in essence resembled the Gascon problem. If France could play the Scottish card, England could play Flanders – and the Empire. There was nothing new in Edward's attempts to build up an anti-French coalition. England had been doing so since the early twelfth century, and was to continue to do so, with interruptions, until the beginning of the nineteenth. But Edward's diplomatic activities in Flanders and Germany were unusually extensive. Among this network of independent and semi-independent principalities, his aims were to secure active help, and troops, if possible, or if not, to arrange neutrality and deny allies to France. He started with the initial advantage that, through his wife, he was connected with three of the leading Flemish potentates; moreover, during this period, he displayed a phenomenal capacity for raising cash on the home and international money-markets: in the late 1330s he was able to borrow – perhaps on the strength of his Scottish victories – over £300,000, far more than any other English medieval sovereign during a comparable period. These funds were laid out with a flourish which impressed every bankrupt Germanic sovereign and freebooter. A score of princes were taken on Edward's payroll. The Duke of Brabant got the huge sum of £60,000. Philippa's rascally brother-in-law, the Emperor Lewis IV – a heretic, a schismatic and an excommunicate – was handsomely paid to provide two thousand men. Edward visited him in state at Coblenz in 1338, where he was invested as the Emperor's vicar-general, which gave him sovereignty in imperial territories west of the Rhine and, in theory at least, the right to exact military service and raise taxes. He took office at Ghent, 'on a throne five foot higher than the rest of those assembled', Philippa by his side, radiating tact and international decorum. Edward also used the leverage of his ability to locate the emporium, or staple, for English wool exports, which meant hard cash for the Flemings; by such manœuvres, he separated the Count of Flanders, whom he could not win over directly, from his leading townsmen, and thus emasculated France's most important potential ally.

These moves were reinforced by administrative reorganisation at home. In 1337, in readiness for war with France, Edward moved his government south from York, and established a dual system by the Walton Ordinances, issued from his port of embarkation on the Naze. These embodied a variety of innovations designed to expedite the collection and transmission of money, but their chief provision was to subject the Chancery and Exchequer (which remained at home) to the authority of the Privy Seal, in the hands of William Kilsby,

Edward and his knights on
horseback during the
French wars.

which was to travel abroad with the King – privy seals being mandatory for Chancery writs and Exchequer payments. Advisory councils were appointed at home and abroad, and the whole superstructure was underwritten by a complex process under which bales of wool were sent direct to the King, for cash sales – their proceeds to finance his operations and service his debts.

Conscious that he was embarking on a hazardous venture, aware that administrative reforms to sustain it might prove unpopular, and above all anxious that his plans should receive the stamp of national approval, Edward took great pains to solicit and obtain the ratification by Parliament of every step which carried him closer to war. Indeed, it can be argued that no English government before – and scarcely any since – has entered war by a fuller process of constitutional assent. A number of council memoranda prepared at the outset of hostilities draw attention to the internal disturbances produced by earlier Anglo-French conflicts, as a result of war taxation; one warned Edward that the burdens imposed by his grandfather would have led to civil war if he had not provided suitable remedies for grievances. During the drift to war, 1336–8, Edward had repeated consultations with Parliamentary assemblies precisely to meet this point; though the Parliament Rolls for these years have not survived, several reliable texts explicitly record that the decision to start the war had been taken by a meeting including both Lords and Commons. Later, in 1343, Edward's spokesman, Bartholomew Burghersh, asked Parliament to debate the desirability of peace negotiations, reminding members that 'this war had been undertaken by the joint assent of the prelates, magnates and commons'. Edward sought, and got, Parliamentary approval for the ends in order to oblige it to vote the means.

But of course he was working with imperfect instruments. Parliament was not yet a body accustomed, or even willing, to participate in the whole process of government: that was the job of the King and his Council. It is significant that the key document, the Walton reforms, was an ordinance, not a statute, and was not submitted to Parliamentary approval. Moreover, it embodied a radical change of precisely the type the English have always resisted – had, indeed, recently resisted

63

under Edward II – the transfer of real power from the traditional organs of state, the Exchequer and Chancery, to a secret office directly attached to the King; and the transfer was made more hateful by the fact that the sea separated the two wings of government. What is more, Edward had introduced this change to fuel an overseas invasion of a magnitude and cost never before undertaken by an English government.

Thus, all Edward's carefully prepared plans broke down virtually from the start. Within a fortnight of his departure, the magnates at home were protesting about the new Exchequer procedure, and theatening a mass-resignation from the Council. More widespread anger was caused by military purveyance, the system whereby the King's officers bought up supplies at fixed prices for transmission to the troops; this was even more unpopular than direct taxation. The situation was made worse by objective economic factors. Good harvests in 1336–8 had produced a glut, leading to low food prices in the year 1338–9, a reduction of acreages, followed by a food shortage and a sharp increase in prices – a familiar cycle. Edward, by his borrowings, had contrived to get a mass of silver which he poured directly into the market, leading to a rapid inflation of goods in short supply. As modern governments know to their cost, attempts to rearm too fast mean simply that they pay more for the same quantity. This is a problem imperfectly understood today, and quite beyond the comprehension of an exasperated fourteenth-century king. Worst of all, the wool needed to keep Edward going came through very slowly, and often in damaged condition. Edward took the customary (and usually futile) step in such circumstances: he appointed a 'strong man' at home, to get things moving. Stratford, the Archbishop of Canterbury, was made 'principal councillor' to the nominal Regent, the future Black Prince, and given sweeping powers to rush over supplies. But Stratford, as the senior English clergyman, was under pressure from papal envoys to make peace, from his brethren to ease clerical taxation and from Parliament to dismantle the injustices of the Walton reforms. By February 1340, Edward had achieved very little in military terms, but his money had run out, and he was trying to borrow it at ruinous rates. He came back, leaving his family behind as security, and at a hastily summoned Parliament, his spokesman announced that the King would have to return to Flanders as a debtor-prisoner, unless fresh supplies were promptly voted. Parliament agreed, but only on condition that a wide spectrum of grievances were removed by statute – abolition of all non-Parliamentary taxes; the end of 'presentment of Englishry', a security device dating from the Conquest which had become an irritating source of royal revenue; reform of the purveyance system; and protection of clerical lands from royal exactions during vacancies.

Thus, at the end of two years of war, Edward had merely saddled himself with a mountain of debt and a constitutional crisis. There was also the problem of national security. French naval plans were maturing. The French had raided Portsmouth and Southampton in 1338, Dover and Folkestone the next year. They had even been in the Thames, and the English were now hastily planting underwater stakes to mine the river approaches to London. Early in the summer of 1340, reports reached Edward that a huge French and Genoese armada was assembling near Sluys, at the mouth of the Zwin, with the object of sweeping English vessels off the sea-lanes and invading the country. Edward was about to return to Flanders himself, but naval intelligence persuaded him to commandeer all available merchant ships, and fill them with pressed and hired troops from all over the Home Counties and the south-east. He rightly grasped that here was an ideal opportunity to strike a major blow at French naval power; we must admire the confidence with which he, a wholly inexperienced naval commander – and a man who suffered, as we know, from seasickness and was afraid of storms – embraced this opportunity to fight a fleet action. But of course his tactics were essentially military: Froissart says that he manned his ships so that each vessel filled with men-at-arms was flanked by two of archers, his invariable procedure on land. The chronicler Adam Murimuth, indeed, describes the Sluys ships as 'wooden horses' – mere vehicles to bring landsmen into close combat. As often under Edward, women were conspicuous in the adventure: he insisted on taking with him – or perhaps they insisted – a great many Court ladies travelling to join the Queen, and he protected them by a force of three hundred men-at-arms and five hundred archers. Edward was fortunate that winds brought him to the scene of

OVERLEAF The battle of Sluys, a great naval victory for Edward's fleet.

65

action while the enemy fleet was still in the Zwin channel. Their numbers caused some dismay – 'so many ships', says Froissart, 'that their masts seemed to be like a great wood'. But Edward, in his cog *Thomas*, had in fact achieved the ideal conditions for his tactics. The French were invited to make a frontal attack in a restricted area which exposed them to the optimum use of the firepower of the English archers. The Genoese admiral, Barbenera, grasped the situation and warned against the dangers of bunching; but he was subordinate to the two Frenchmen, Admirals Quieret and Behuchet, themselves sharing a divided command, and a mass frontal attack was ordered – exactly what Edward hoped for. It was midsummer day, the wind and tide in England's favour and the sun in their enemies' faces. Barbenera's galleys were largely independent of the elements, and he and most of his squadron contrived to escape. The rest of the French fleet was virtually destroyed, and both admirals killed.

Sluys ended the threat of French invasion, gave the English command of the sea-lanes, at least for a time, and enormously enhanced Edward's reputation. But it did nothing to further his attempt to strike at the heart of French military power. From Flanders, he wrote a triumphant account of the victory to his infant son, the Regent, which has been rightly described as the earliest English naval despatch. But he still had no cash to unleash land-warfare, and at the end of September he accepted a nine-month truce. He had wanted a quick, decisive battle, which Philip had prudently declined, knowing that time worked against the English forces, dependent on long lines of communication, and short of money and supplies. Edward brooded on his missed opportunities, placing the blame squarely on the incompetence and pusillanimity of the civil admini-stration at home. In fact, there was little it could do, for the supplies voted by Parliament had been pre-empted by his Italian bankers and other creditors. But Edward's customary affability was yielding to a spasm of Plantagenet wrath – directed, in particular, at Stratford and other clerical ministers. He was surrounded by angry men of action, of his own generation, or a little older, eager for military glamour – egged on, indeed, by their womenfolk – and thirsting for plunder and ransoms; they thought, and Edward thought, that they were being frustrated by elderly bishops at home, who did not even believe in the war. Perhaps Edward had a personal animus against Stratford, the origins of which are unknown to us; at any rate, on 18 November 1340 he wrote to the Pope at Avignon, accusing the Archbishop of a variety of offences, some clearly imaginary. But basically the crisis arose from a conflict of generation – 'He listened,' says Murimuth, 'to the council of young men, spurning the advice of the older ones' – and, in particular, a conflict between what the early twentieth century would call 'the brasshats' and 'the frocks' – fighting men in the front line exasperated by gabbling, do-nothing politicians at home. Edward's remedy sprang from this atmosphere: he would repeat his *coup* against Mortimer at Nottingham, by a swift, decisive and secret personal intervention. He announced officially that he would spend Christmas at Ghent; then, with only 'eight of his followers, pretending that he wished to go out for a ride, he left secretly, without warning even his household staff, and came to Sluys, where he set sail'. He reached the Tower by water, at dawn on 30 November, and caught its Constable, Sir Nicholas Beche, absent without leave. Rockets and thunderbolts rained down in wondrous fashion. The Constable, five senior judges, officials and merchants were arrested; writs for summary proceedings were dispatched and prosecuted with vigour; great severity was exercised against officials high and low, who were forced to buy their freedom by huge sureties. Stratford retired hastily to Canterbury and his two episcopal brother-ministers were dismissed, being replaced by laymen. Edward stated flatly that in future his ministers must be answerable in his own courts and unprotected by clerical privilege.

This drastic purge set up panic tremors throughout the English body politic, especially in the powerful clerical section of it. Edward had to learn the hard way that England was a civil country, where the martial methods of the Continent, however necessary they might seem in wartime, were wholly unacceptable. The English clergy were not popular with the public; but they were formidable opponents when they contrived to align clerical rights with civil liberties, and represent both as equally threatened by a tyrannous executive. And this was precisely what Stratford – a poor administrator but no

OPPOSITE Edward III, flanked by bishops and courtiers, receives a book from Walter de Milemete.

68

pistola allectuia
chim rege ad saenci
e regalis cognicioñe.
Xcellentissimo il
lustcelmo suo · dommo edlkar
w dinina pinsione · regi ang

A fourteenth-century
ivory chessman of a bishop.

mean publicist – set out to do. He invoked the great English
shibboleth, Magna Carta, and threatened to excommunicate
any royal official who broke it. He invoked Thomas Becket,
his trump card, and preached a sensational sermon in English
at Canterbury, on 29 December, the anniversary of Becket's
martyrdom. Edward laid charges against him; he replied with
a manifesto, which provoked counter-manifestos, and Parliament finally met in April 1341 in a welter of political
propaganda. The Archbishop undoubtedly got the better of
the argument, disarming the forces of anti-clericalism which
Edward arrayed against him by showing that royal abuses
against the clergy were paralleled by abuses against laymen of
all degrees – and he was believed, for government exactions
were currently more obvious than clerical ones. Parliament

70

demolished the Walton Ordinances, and Edward accepted its verdict.

Indeed, the King learned a number of lessons. He drew back from the brink of a Church–State conflict which must have harmed both sides and impeded the war-effort. Stratford responded. Both men, fortunately, were by nature conciliators, and patriots in their different ways. Edward did not want to be a Henry II, and certainly the Archbishop had no aspirations to martyrdom. By October 1341 they were reconciled, and Stratford once more became chief councillor. Parliament, and the Commons in particular, moved closer to the centre of the political stage. Henceforth, its control over taxation steadily tightened. But it did not seek and Edward did not need to concede, its control over the executive. Parliament was not a permanent body, but a safety-valve for discontent in moments of crisis; it required gestures of consultation, which Edward was happy, and supremely able, to supply. After 1341, for thirty years, his relations with Parliament remained comparatively easy, without any real sacrifice of his prerogative. His quarrel with Stratford was his first and last showdown with a senior member of the establishment – he learned that lesson, too. And he accepted the basic conservatism of the English by abandoning his attempts at administrative reform and returning to the traditional instruments of the Chancery and the Exchequer. Edward III finally came of age in 1341.

Thus the English muddled themselves out of a constitutional breakdown, as they were accustomed to do. What is more surprising, they muddled themselves out of Edward's appalling financial difficulties. In the 1340s, his Italian bankers were abandoned to their fate as broken instruments: the Peruzzi, owed £77,000 plus interest, collapsed in 1343; the Bardi, owed £103,000, followed three years later: local financial syndicates were assembled, and milked in turn; the last went bankrupt in 1349. After 1353 the King could no longer borrow money at all, but by then he had secured the services of William Edington, Bishop of Winchester, a brilliant financier who served the King for over twenty-three years, as Keeper of the Wardrobe, Treasurer of the Exchequer and Chancellor: he saw Edward through all his great campaigns. The fact is, royal revenue, properly administered, was expanding, thanks to Edward's

successful efforts to promote the cloth trade and his ability to conciliate Parliament. It paid the state not to borrow money. There were the windfalls of war: royal ransoms (of the kings of Scotland and France) brought in £286,000, at a time at which annual state revenue was around the £60,000-mark. Of course, there were many anxious moments. Both Edward and his son, the Black Prince, appear to have bought jewelry in good times, so that it could be hocked in bad. Successive inventories of the royal jewels and regalia tell the story. The Great Crown was first in hock in 1334, redeemed the next year, pledged again in 1340 and redeemed at the end of the decade. Inventories of 1356, 1361 and 1367 reveal that it was at the pawnbrokers for nearly fifteen years. On the other hand, new crowns were made, one as late as 1367. The fundamental financial position of the state remained sound until the onset of Edward's dotage. Indeed, in the period 1362–70, the Exchequer was full enough to advance loans of £31,000 itself. During the middle years of his reign, Edward was able to wage war – and enjoy peace when it came – against a background of comparative political and financial stability. For this, his willingness to compromise and his equable temperament were mainly responsible. He had become a characteristic English statesman.

OPPOSITE A majestic figure at the west door of Lincoln Cathedral, believed to represent Edward III.

4 High Noon 1341-50

...les raisons que le prince de
...lles remonstra ce iour a ses
...ns et fist par ses mareschaulx
...monstrer ilz furent tous re
...nfortez. Delez le prince pour
...garder et conseillier estoit
...essire Jehan chandos ne oncqs

PREVIOUS PAGES
Decorative detail from a
page of Froissart's
Chronicles. Jean Froissart
was a poet and chronicler
born at Valenciennes in
Hainault in about 1337. In
1361 he went to England
and became secretary and
man of letters to Queen
Philippa, until her death in
1369. Froissart wrote long
narrative love poems in the
courtly tradition but is best
remembered for the
Chronicles which record
events in Western Europe
from 1325 to 1400.

IT WAS ONE THING to back the war-effort by a sound civil
administration at home; quite another to solve the strategic
problems the war raised. If Edward failed to campaign actively
in France, his position in Gascony went by default: that was quite
clear. He had to bring the French to decisive battle and destroy
their capacity to continue the struggle; but the French were well
aware of this, conscious throughout that time worked in their
favour provided they avoided military calamity. It was no use
Edward planting an army in Flanders unless he possessed the
numbers and supplies which allowed it to range freely through
the French countryside for long periods, destroying villages and
towns and drying up French royal revenue. In this way he could
confront the French with a choice between unacceptable
economic sacrifices or the risks of pitched battle. But to place,
and keep, such an English army in the field required a mighty
war-organisation.

The chronicles describe the war in terms of individual
heroism. The state papers tell a more prosaic story. During the
reign of Edward's grandfather, the feudal organisation of
warfare had finally collapsed. It had never been possible in
England to create effective armies on the basis of knight-services
provided by tenants-in-chief; monetary compensation for
military service, the scutage, had not worked either – attempts
to exact it had brought King John to his knees at Runnymede.
Edward I had evolved a wholly professional, paid army, based
on contracts of service with leading magnates and knights.
Edward III brought the system to completion: under him, all
ranks were paid, from Edward Balliol, titular King of Scots,
who got 50s a day, and the Black Prince, who got 20s, down to
Cheshire archers and Flintshire lancers, who were paid 2d. By
1341 written contracts were well established: an individual
captain contracted to supply x men for y days at z wages,
payment being directly liened to a portion of a wool subsidy or
other tax. Later, commanders accepted responsibility for a
specific assignment, for a specific period. These contracts went
into considerable detail, for example over compensation for
lost horses (the King paid out £6,656 under this head between
July 1338 and May 1340). Some companies still reflected the
household structures of great magnates. But boroughs and
shires were expected to fulfil ancient obligations to provide

manpower through Commissions of Array. Able-bodied men were paraded locally, and selected for service by provost-marshals. Local authorities provided equipment; but there was fierce argument as to who should pay the men before they reached ports of embarkation, when the King automatically picked up the bill. Money determined all, for a man could buy his way out of the draft. In fact, pressing was operated on a large scale only in times of sudden emergency. We hear of no complaints of compulsion, though local communities were vociferous in protest against paying expenses. Villages and towns used the array to get rid of local riffraff, and the gaols were emptied if necessary. Falstaff's ruffianly crew in *Henry IV Part 1* was already adumbrated in the reign of Edward III; indeed the system had changed little by Elizabethan times. In any case, there were always plenty of volunteers, attracted by high rates of pay and the prospect of plunder; for his 1359 expedition, Edward had many more than he could handle. Horses were a much bigger problem for him. As plate armour became more elaborate and heavier, bigger horses were required; they were always in short supply – losses were appalling – and the price rose in proportion. Edward paid £120 for a *destrier*, or war-horse, as early as 1331; a good one cost £200 by the end of the reign, and his agents scoured as far afield as Sicily and Spain to buy them.

The creation of a professional army had obvious advantages, not least that Edward could choose his captains on merit, and promote them accordingly. Formations varied enormously in size, though the standard unit averaged a hundred. We know little about uniforms, but green and white were the standard colours for the Welsh and Cheshire troops who formed the bulk of Edward's rank and file. Though the army was professional, it was also hierarchic: Edward always ensured that it reflected the social structure of the realm. Career officers commanded the smaller units, but the larger formations were in the hands of the higher nobility; true, as the war progressed, Edward promoted low-born captains who had distinguished themselves, but only those who had acquired wealth and set up as landed proprietors. One example was Walter Manny, a brilliant Flemish soldier who came to England in Philippa's retinue and died rich and a knight of the Garter; another was

A brass rubbing of the effigy of William de Aldeburgh, c. 1360, showing the style of armour in Edward's reign.

Sir Hugh Calveley, a Cheshire peasant who ended as Governor of Brest and a magnate of his county; he built and endowed a fine collegiate church in Bunbury, to house his costly tomb. Those successful captains who could adjust to their changed status and abide by upper-class conventions were admitted to the elite. But, in general, Edward chose his generals from among his friends, and was well served. The men who fought with him as commanders on his first campaigns – Henry, Earl of Derby, the Earls of Warwick, Suffolk and Northampton – were with him to the last. The King was a good picker of officers; we hear no reports of quarrels or dissensions. He knew how to inspire the ranks, too; discipline and morale remained high, even in the most desperate and gruesome circumstances. No mutinies are recorded.

The core of the army was the man-at-arms, who almost invariably fought dismounted. Getting him into his armour was an elaborate business. He wore no shirt but a fustian doublet lined with satin cut full of holes for ventilation; he was literally sewn into this garment, with fine twine of the kind used for crossbows, covered in shoemaker's wax; gussets of mail were sewn onto it at the bend of the arm and under the arm, to cover gaps in the plate-mail. Then he put on worsted hose, with blanket-pads around the knees to prevent chafing by the armour, and thick leather shoes fastened with whipcord. Next came sabatons (foot armour) tied to his shoes, greaves (leg armour), cuisses (thigh armour), a mail breach to protect his genitals, tonlets (laminated skirts to protect the stomach), a breastplate, vambraces on the forearms and rerebraces on the upper arms; finally armoured gloves. His dagger hung on his right side, short sword on his left, a surcoat on his back. Then his bascinet or helmet was put on and fastened with buckles front and back. Lastly, his long sword was put into his right hand, and his pennant into his left. The business of arming was so elaborate that men often slept in their armour on campaign. Rain was the supreme enemy – as in the Flanders of 1917 – for it turned the field into mud, and a man-at-arms, once down, quickly suffocated.

Dismounted men-at-arms were flanked by archers using the longbow. Edward had two hundred mounted archers, from Cheshire, who served as his personal bodyguard; they were

RIGHT Archery practice from the Luttrell Psalter *c.* 1340. Parliament passed repeated statutes forbidding village games such as dice, football and cockfighting because they distracted the villagers from archery.

BELOW Longbows (left) confronting crossbows. The advantage of the longbow was in its quick rate of fire whereas the crossbow had to be drawn back by a small winch which sometimes jammed.

expensive troops, paid 6d a day, whose light horses gave them great mobility. But of course they shot on foot, for accuracy. The overwhelming majority of the archers were footmen; they carried pointed stakes, which were placed in rows in front of their position to protect them from cavalry. The French never developed the longbow as a weapon, and the reason is not hard to discover. It required immense skill to use effectively, and this could be developed only by long years of training at a local level. French peasants were forbidden to possess arms, and the law was largely enforced. In England it had broken down – if it had ever been observed – in the twelfth century. English peasants were not only permitted, they were positively commanded by the state to train at archery; indeed they trained in village formations. In the fourteenth century, Parliament passed repeated statutes forbidding other forms of village entertain-

ment – those mentioned included tennis, dice, football (regarded as particularly abhorrent because it led to hooliganism and riots, as today), quoits, handball, various forms of cricket and hockey classed as 'club-ball', cock-fighting and 'other games of no value': anything, in short, which diverted men from archery.

Training manuals which have survived describe in great detail how to use the longbows. They were made of yew, maple and oak, and by the 1350s were six feet in length. Their range was four hundred yards and they could penetrate chain-mail. What made them so superior to the crossbow was their rate of fire, five to six times as great; a trained longbowman could dispatch an arrow every five seconds. Unlike the crossbow, they had no complicated machinery to jam in action, and they were light enough for the archer to carry several in case the string broke. Faced with advancing cavalry, the longbowmen, firing in alterate ranks, aimed in the first place at the horses; if they could bring the front rank floundering down, the charge was as good as broken (the tactic was not all that different from Wellington's squares at Waterloo: the principle of firepower was the same). Dismounted men in armour had a better chance of getting through. But they could charge only short distances on foot. Even so, they had to move fast, with their armoured heads down to deflect the arrows. On a hot day, the temptation to lift the visor or remove the gorget was great; then the English archers immediately shot at the unprotected face and neck. Whenever possible, the archers were placed at the top of slopes, to make the advancing men-at-arms tire faster. If the French got close enough to the archers to use their weapons, the English men-at-arms on the flanks moved in. Behind the archers, too, were Welsh footmen, armed with knives. These were military scavengers, the lowest form of the hierarchy, but deadly once an armoured man was wounded, or fell, slipping their blades in between his plates. Such tactics were denounced as unchivalrous, but were invariably employed.

Where the English were weakest was in siege-warfare. The age of the cannon was only just dawning. The English first used 'crakys of war' against the Scots in 1327, and six years later Edward himself had 'gounes' at the siege of Berwick. Initially imported, both guns and gunpowder were soon being manufactured at home: the earliest Chamber and Issue Rolls show purchases of sulphur and saltpetre in 1333–5. They continued to be bought in growing quantity for making up into gunpowder at the Tower; and in 1345 Edward ordered the casting of *ribaldi*, or small cannon, before crossing to France. They may have been used at Crécy, but chiefly to frighten the French horses; they were certainly in use at Calais, and by the end of the reign, Froissart records, the English had as many as a hundred cannon and mortars at the siege of St Malo. But as siege guns, the weapons available to Edward were still more for show than effect. It was an age in which, in both field and fort, the advantage lay decisively with the defence.

Evidence about the size of Edward's armies is conflicting. Chroniclers normally overestimate the size of medieval armies, though sometimes they underrate them for artistic effect. Froissart says that Edward had 3,000 men-at-arms and 5,200

82

archers at Crécy, but he was anxious to emphasise the brilliance of the victory. The accounts of Walter Wetwang, Keeper of the Wardrobe, covering April 1344–November 1347, and letters to England from one of Edward's clerks, Michael de Northburg, show that the forces were larger. Wetwang's lists give a total of 32,303 in the King's pay overseas. There were 5,340 men-at-arms, and over 16,000 foot-archers, plus innumerable workmen. But it is not clear how many of these were on detached service in Gascony and Brittany. In any case, the size of armies was often in inverse proportion to their effectiveness. Control in battle was all-important – it was Edward's great strength, as was his skill in choosing ground and deploying units to suit it. A disciplined, well-placed force could ensure that only a small proportion of the enemy could be brought into action, and once the first attacking wave was repulsed – provided the front was narrow enough – numbers became a positive disadvantage, and a mighty host could quickly be turned into a stampeding mob.

Nonetheless, no English forces of this size had been sent abroad before; shipping and then supplying them required prodigies of organisation. Edward tried to keep morale high by feeding his men well, if at all possible. They ate beef, mutton, salted pork, oats, beans, peas, cheese, dried fish and wheat bread, and they drank ale. Much of the food was brought from England and carried with the armies, for it was often impossible to live off a devastated land. Royal purveyors had the right to buy food in advance of competitors, to demand 'heaped' instead of 'raised' measure, to pay with tallies (cash payments were sometimes two years behind), and, through the sheriffs, to commandeer carriage, of waggons, horses, barges and boats. Virtually the whole country was organised behind the expeditions, on a geographical basis. The 1346 expedition was supplied from Yorkshire, via the Ouse and the Trent to Hull; from Lincolnshire and Boston to King's Lynn; from Norfolk to Yarmouth; from Suffolk to the Orwell; from Essex to Maldon. Goods were loaded in ships and taken to Portsmouth, from Oxford and Bedforshire down the Thames to London, from Kent *via* Sandwich and from the West *via* Bristol. Broadly speaking, the east ports served the Flanders forces, Portsmouth those in Normandy, Plymouth and Bristol those in Aquitaine.

The Machinery of Siege Warfare

During the French wars the reduction of towns by siege was as important as the winning of battles. Edward took siege engines abroad in pieces to be assembled on arrival. Despite the ingenuity of the weapons available, towns more frequently fell to starvation than to direct attack.

RIGHT (left to right) A machine for throwing balls of Greek fire from a rotating windmill structure; a ballistra loaded with round stone is wound up by a capstan; a knight aims a fire missile from a large crossbow.

OPPOSITE A windlass and capstan aims darts at the door of a castle;
LEFT A catapult;
BELOW LEFT A cannon.

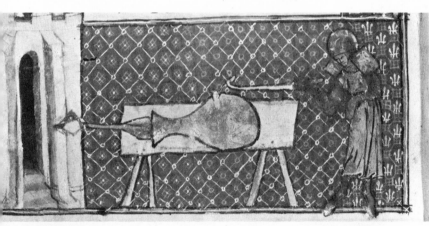

estimo iq qual facere mtrudus in
multishmali casibs prnm ani
mitm delibzatum edispn enedu

85

Transports were commandeered merchant ships; sometimes Edward seized them loaded, discharged the cargo, then sailed them empty to the embarcation points. They varied from thirty to three hundred tons. Whenever possible he took his siege engines on board; otherwise he shipped the materials, for assembly on the spot. Sometimes he rebuilt ships with enlarged gangways to load horses and waggons. Few ports had quays or windlasses; only Sandwich had a dock. The crossing to Calais could be made in a single day, to Normandy in three; Bordeaux might take ten or eleven. We hear of few reports of shipwreck, though the weather often kept expeditions in harbour, or even led to their abandonment. But in 1341 Edward presented a golden ship to his father's shrine, in thanksgiving for survival from a storm.

This great war-effort served essentially a defensive purpose. Edward may or may not have believed in his claim to the French throne. His secret diplomatic instructions suggest that he was always prepared to relinquish it in exchange for solid concessions. Of course, he had to convince the English public that it was genuine, and international opinion that he was righteous. His propaganda was relentless and unyielding. But he probably saw the wars as essentially a holding operation, to maintain the *status quo*. In this sense, despite the reverses of his last years, he succeeded. Although the high hopes raised at one time proved illusory, the English position in France when he died was no worse than when he came to the throne, and in some respects better, for the English possession of Calais was an important military and commercial gain. The net effect of Edward's war was to postpone England's expulsion from France for half a century; we might not see this as a desirable object, but contemporary opinion thought otherwise.

During the 1340s, the war spread rapidly, and eventually involved a great part of western Europe. It soon became clear that the attempt to crush France from the basis of a Flanders coalition was too expensive and, in any event, would not work. The Emperor Lewis was bribed into the French camp, and Edward's vicariate terminated. A succession of French popes – two actually from the areas in dispute – strove vigorously to bring about a peace which must favour France. Edward had to enlarge the sphere of conflict, by probing for fresh weaknesses in the French position. In 1342 he seized eagerly on a disputed succession in Brittany, backing one of the claimants, John de Montfort, who came to Windsor to swear allegiance to Edward as King of France, and was made Earl of Richmond. Philip VI backed Charles of Blois, the rival claimant, and invaded the province. English troops under Manny, and another adventurer, Sir Thomas Dagworth, were despatched, and Edward took an army there himself, but he could not bring the French to battle, and signed a truce in January 1343. It was important to the English to secure ports in Brittany to protect their routes to Bordeaux; but to ravage the Breton countryside inflicted no harm on the French Crown.

It was a different matter with Normandy. By the early summer of 1346, Edward had collected an army in Portsmouth to relieve the southern front of Aquitaine. At the last moment, according to Froissart, a French exile, Geoffrey de Harcourt, persuaded him to attack Normandy:

> Sir, the country of Normandy is one of the most plenteous countries in the world ... if you will land there, there is none that shall resist you; the people of Normandy have not been used to war ... and you shall find great towns that have not been walled, and your men will be rich for twenty years after. ...

Whether Edward's strategy was determined in such a haphazard manner seems unlikely; certainly, it made military sense to extend the conflict to what might be called, at that date, France's soft over-belly. At all events, Edward landed at St Vaast-de-la-Hogue on 12 July, planning to ravage in a north-east direction, and eventually to join up with his Flemish forces. The object was to inflict economic damage and, if possible, force Philip into battle.

We have a very detailed description from Froissart of the manner in which Edward set about this strategy, with the Bishop of Durham as his spiritual adviser, and the Earls of Warwick, Arundel and Northampton as his chief lieutenants. His first act on landing was to knight his sixteen-year-old son, Edward, and create him Prince of Wales. Next he sent his fleet on a north-east course along the coast, with instructions to burn all undefended or lightly-defended ports. After spending the night in La Hogue, and burning it the next morning, he moved

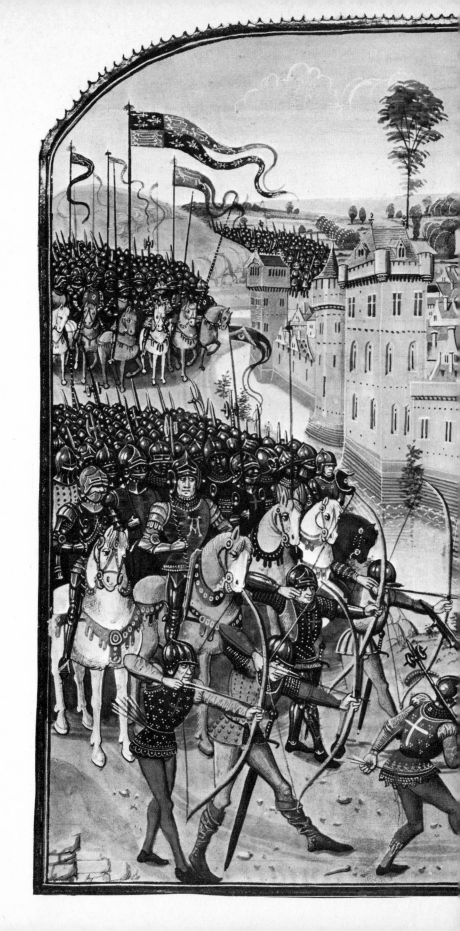

The taking of Caen by the
English army.

inland in a leisurely fashion. He spent five days in the Cotentin, 'during which the whole countryside and coast was devastated and the town of Barfleur was burnt'. He crossed the Douve, and stormed Caen after a fierce fight on the bridge (it was evidently unwalled), where three thousand citizens were killed and a number of valuable persons captured and despatched to England to await ransom; the booty so far collected was also loaded on home-bound ships. Edward stormed a number of towns and castles situated on the march which were ill-equipped to withstand siege; but he by-passed towns such as Vernon and Beauvais which had high walls and strong garrisons. He was evidently anxious to economise effort (and time) and strike only where the French were weakest. Abbeys and priories were not spared, and among the prisoners was the Abbess of Caen. Edward received a papal peace mission, led by two cardinals and an archbishop, but he refused even to negotiate the terms they offered, and the risks he took crossing the Seine and the Somme make it clear that he was aiming, all the time, to tempt Philip to battle.

Philip may well have wished to avoid battle entirely, allow Edward to complete his mission and slip away. The French army, though growing daily as contingents arrived from all over France, seems to have been ill-organised and ill-disciplined, and it had never trained, let alone operated, as a body. At Abbeville, on 25 August, Edward offered battle, but Philip declined, and after waiting for him throughout the night, Edward moved north to Crécy. Philip might still have hesitated, but his grip on his army was slack, and he was under intense pressure from his leading commanders to attack: 'so confident were the French leaders in the size of their army that they asked for particular Englishmen to be allotted to them as prisoners'. Leading the war-party was the King of Bohemia, Philip's experienced and bellicose ally, who insisted on being given command of the leading French division; it was his impetuosity, rather than any deliberate plan of the French King, which determined the timing and course of the battle.

Although innumerable historians have made sketch-maps of Crécy, they are based on imaginative guess-work; none of the accounts we have provides the kind of detail necessary to reconstruct the actual placing and movement of units on either side. What can be said is that Edward put himself in a defensive position, with the town of Crécy in his rear, thick woods on his right and the River Maie on his left: these two obstacles narrowed the front he had to defend, and they converged near Crécy itself, so that the further the French advanced, the more they would lose their freedom of manœuvre – a classic Edwardian disposition. He commanded the third division, or reserve, which gave him the maximum opportunity to observe and control the course of the battle, Arundel and Northampton the centre division, and the young Prince, assisted by experienced lieutenant-generals, the vanguard. Each English division had men-at-arms at the centre, flanked by massed archers.

Whether Philip gave the actual order to attack we do not know. The only decisive action Froissart attributes to him is the command not to take prisoners for ransom, symbolised by unfurling the Oriflamme. The sun had already set before he decided to fight. The action began with an advance of some seven thousand of his crossbowmen, many of them Italian mercenaries. As the maximum distance they could shoot was about a hundred yards, none of them got within range of the first English division before they were cut down by English arrows, and broke. At that point, the French commanders lost whatever control of the battle they had possessed. The leading French division of mounted men-at-arms, furious at the failure and impotence of their bowmen, charged without orders straight at the English lines, riding down their own men, who were crushed beneath the horses. Once through this mêlée, the French cavalry were still two hundred yards from the English line, and a wave of arrows brought down the front rank of their horses. In the growing darkness, those at the rear of the French army could not see what was happening at the front. The screams of terror and pain coming from the crossbowmen and horses convinced them that a general battle had been joined, and all the rear cavalry divisions surged forward, slamming into the first division, which was now retreating. The darkness made it difficult for the English archers to shoot accurately: they simply aimed at the struggling mass of men and horses in front. Some French men-at-arms, on foot, reached the English vanguard. The young Prince was engaged in fierce hand-to-hand fighting, and at one point was down on his knees. But by

The French crossbows
oppose the English
longbows at the battle of
Crécy.

the time a group of twenty knights, despatched by Edward to
get him out of trouble, reached the Prince, they found him and
his men 'leaning on lances and swords, taking breath and
resting quietly on long mounds of corpses, waiting for the
enemy who had withdrawn'. In all, says Froissart, the French
charged fifteen times during the night, and again, with four
fresh divisions, at dawn. But the English tactical position was
by now unassailable, protected by barriers of French dead,
across which the bowmen shot with impunity. Daylight
showed an appalling scene of dead and dying horses and men –
four thousand knights and 'men of superior dignity', says
Froissart, were killed, almost all on the French side; 'no one
troubled to count the others who were slain'. Among the dead
were the King of Bohemia, whose feathered crest and motto,
Ich Dien, the Prince appropriated, the Count of Flanders, the
Duke of Lorraine, nine French counts – 'and German counts

whose names are not known' – an archbishop, an abbot, the Prior of the Knights of St John of Jerusalem, and a bishop; Philip also lost the Marshal of his army – no great misfortune, one would think – and his leading political counsellor. English losses are given as forty. The body of the Bohemian King was washed in warm water and wrapped in clean linen; the next day, the Bishop of Durham celebrated a solemn requiem Mass for the repose of his soul, and of the other dead. Then Edward and his army moved north, investing Calais on 4 September.

The names of those present at Crécy emphasise the international character of the conflict: France, in particular, was organising her resources throughout north-west Europe, and even in central Europe, Italy and Spain. After Crécy, Philip was unable to strike back himself, but he persuaded his young Scottish ally, King David, to break the 1345 truce and invade England. Our chief account of this campaign, the Lanercost Chronicle, is extraordinarily confused, its monkish author jumbling together bombast, English propaganda and irritating Latin puns, as well as fascinating and authentic detail. But evidently David's intelligence was at fault; he assumed, or had been told, that all the north of England had been stripped bare of troops for Edward's French expedition. In fact, whatever disposition Edward had to make in France, he was always careful to ensure that the 'postern gate' was well-guarded. He raised no troops from the north for his Crécy campaign, and the levies from the four northern counties, under Neville and Percy, the wardens of the Marches, were promptly enlisted when the truce was broken, and an army assembled at York under the command of its archbishop, William de la Zouche. It marched north, and near Durham, at Neville's Cross, came into contact with the Scottish army in a thick fog. The Lanercost description tells us nothing about the battle, except that the Scots were defeated and many of them slain: presumably English discipline and firepower were decisive. Chivalry played little part in these Scottish campaigns. Before the battle, an English Franciscan bishop exhorted the troops to take no Scotch prisoners. In fact, a good many were captured – including King David – and one of them, the Earl of Menteith, was charged with treason, tried in London, hanged, drawn and quartered, his limbs being sent to various towns in England and Scotland. David was reserved

Coment le roy Dauid
descocie vint atout grāt ost
deuant le neufchusteau
sur thyne. ⁊ le siege chū

The capture of King David II of Scotland outside Newcastle upon Tyne.

et toute la deftruction que
le roy eduart et les anglois
auoient faicte en escoce

for a huge ransom and imprisoned in Windsor Castle.

With Philip and the Scots temporarily crushed, Edward could afford to take his time over Calais. He needed a deep-water base on the French coast, both to strengthen his grip on the sea-lanes and to act as a bridgehead for future expeditions; he may also have already planned to set up the wool-staple there. But he had no intention of losing men on a direct assault. Calais had a double-ditch, fed by tidal seawater, and very high double walls. In the fourteenth century, storming a well-built and strongly garrisoned town was an immensely costly operation, which could easily end in complete failure. This fact helps to explain the extraordinary ferocity with which the inhabitants of towns taken by assault were sometimes treated. A walled town was a military as well as a commercial unit; men were encouraged by the Crown to settle there for precisely this purpose, and could not expect to be regarded solely as civilians. Medieval laws of war, such as they were, limited non-combatants to clergy and peasants going about their business. Townsmen were at risk. It was considered fair that a town which had been effectively invested by a superior army should surrender; if it failed to do so, and forced the besiegers to risk assault, its citizens exposed themselves to whatever punishment the victor felt desirable, when and if the town was taken. Jean de Vienne, the brave but invalid Governor of Calais (he was a martyr to gout), knew the rules perfectly well. By refusing to yield the town, he was banking on a relieving expedition by Philip; if this failed to show up, the town must eventually fall, he and his leading colleagues would probably be hanged and lesser fry massacred.

Edward's investment of Calais lasted over a year. It was a very costly business. He commanded the sea, and effectively blockaded the town, but his fleet was exposed to attack by Norman privateers, who captured or burned fifteen of his ships during the siege. He could not use siege engines against the walls, says the Baker chronicle, because the ground was too soft. All he could do was to surround the town with trenches, and wait for its supplies to run out. This carried the risk of epidemic, the frequent fate of besieging forces in medieval times. But the morale of his troops remained high during the long months of waiting: Edward was a popular commander

Dant le roy sceut
ces nouuelles z
la certamete du
iiour qui arieste y
estoit. il se partit dangletre
auec. iii. hommes darmes
et. vi. archiers et mota sur
mer ou port de douures. et
sur vng vespre il arriua a
calais tout secretemet q̃
on nen sceut riens. Et se
buchierent ses homme. ou
chasteau en chambres z
en tours et le roy aussi q̃

dist au s̃. de mauny. Messc
gaultier ie vueil que vous
soyes de ceste besoigne chief
z souuerain. car moyz mo
filz nous combatras soubz
vre baniere. Or diray de
messire gieffroy de charny
qui le derrain iour de dece
bre se partit duras auec
ses gens darmes archiers z
arbalestriers Et sen vint
bien pres de calais enuiron
my nuit. Si sarresta en
atendant ses ges et ceuoiz

The Hundred Years' War

The English possession of the duchy of Aquitaine brought a permanent tension into Anglo-French relations which was magnified by Edward's claim to the French throne and the fear of a French alliance with Scotland. In 1329 Edward paid homage to Philip VI (left) but no differences were settled. In 1338 Edward invaded France in the first of the series of campaigns which made up the Hundred Years' War.

BELOW The siege of Tournai by the English army.
OPPOSITE BELOW The battle of Crécy.

Ladies at the bedside of the sleeping king. Edward enjoyed feminine company and usually made provision for Queen Philippa and the other wives to accompany his expeditions.

primarily because he did not commit his men to action unless circumstances (more important than numerical odds) were heavily in their favour. Serving in his army was a comparatively safe occupation. He did his best to make things comfortable. Wooden huts were built for the men, Flemish traders invited, markets held twice a week, wives – including his own – brought across.

Froissart and his chief source Jean le Bel are the only chroniclers who mention Philippa's presence, but there is no good reason to disbelieve them. Froissart was later attached to Philippa's household and probably got an eye-witness account from her own lips. If he treats her as the heroine, her behaviour as described by him was very much in character. Edward liked to have his womenfolk around him whenever possible, and play the agreeable masculine role of a severe disciplinarian whose heart could be touched by feminine pleas. He took a big risk at Calais, but there was always the chance that Philip would be forced into a second, decisive, encounter, and even fall prisoner. If, on the other hand, the French King failed to relieve Calais, the prestige of his crown would suffer, notably in Gascony and Brittany, and marginal men would shift their allegiances. This was another object of Edward's strategy. As it happened, long before Calais fell, Sir Thomas Dagworth, now commanding in Brittany, won a notable victory at La Roche-Derrien, and the French claimant, Charles of Blois, was taken; two out of Edward's three principal enemies were now in his hands. The collapse of his position in Brittany affected Philip's hesitant strategy in the north; in August, after manœuvring for some time near Edward's lines, Philip declined battle and withdrew, compelling Jean de Vienne to surrender. Unable to walk,

The capture of Charles of Blois at La Roche-Derrien.

101

he rode out of the gates on a horse, a rope round his neck; the chief knights and burghers, also roped, followed on foot. Philippa, if we are to believe Froissart, persuaded Edward to spare their lives; Baker says that they were taken to England for ransom. Otherwise, Calais was severely treated: the entire population was moved out to Guines and all property confiscated; settlers were moved in from England, and a ring of forts built in the march. Calais became an English plantation, base and *entrepôt*, and remained one for over two hundred years.

The 1340s were years of victory for Edward, though the coming of the Black Death in 1349 brought confusion and a temporary end to active campaigning. After Calais, says the chronicler Walsingham, the English thought that a new sun had risen 'because of the abundance of peace in England' – he means, of course, security from foreign or domestic peril – 'the plenitude of goods and the glory of the victories'; there was hardly a woman in England who was not wearing spoils from Caen, Calais and other French towns. After Crécy, recorded the Parliament Roll, the Lords and Commons passed motions formally thanking God 'for the victory that He had granted to their liege-lord ... and said that all the money they had given him had been well spent'. Edward was 'our cumly king', the 'famous and fortunate warrior'; since he came to the throne 'the realm of England has been nobly amended, honoured and enriched to a degree never seen in the time of any other king'. This hyperbole was echoed throughout Europe, where Edward was now regarded as the greatest man of his time. 'When the noble Edward first gained England in his youth', wrote Jean le Bel, 'nobody thought much of the English, nobody spoke of their prowess and courage. ... Now, in the time of the noble Edward, who has often put them to the test, they are the finest and most daring warriors known to man.'

Edward rounded off the decade, in August 1350, with a striking naval victory off Winchelsea against the Castilian galleys, commanded by Admiral Charles de la Cerda. Castile was the great naval power of the future, and already formidable. Though France and England were now at truce, and Flanders supposedly neutral, the Castilians continued to use Sluys as a base for raids against English shipping, and the fleet which Edward assembled at Sandwich was primarily defensive. He

A ship of war, *c.* 1340.

sailed in his favourite cog *Thomas* – called, of course, after the archbishop murdered by his great-great-great-grandfather – and took with him not only the Black Prince but his younger brother, the ten-year-old John of Gaunt. Froissart gives a delightful description of Edward at sea:

The King stood at his ship's prow, clad in a jacket of black velvet, and on his head a hat of black beaver which was very becoming; and he was then (as I was told by those who were with him) as merry as ever he was seen. He made his minstrels play a German dance which had lately been brought to England by Lord John Chandos, who was present; and for fun he made this knight sing with the minstrels and was delighted at the result. And at times he would look upwards, for he had set a watch in the topcastle of his ship to give warning of the Spaniards' coming.

103

Fourteenth-century
daggers.

When the galleys were sighted, the King ordered wine all round, and then put on his armour. He and his sons were in considerable danger, for the Spanish ships were equipped with catapults hurling iron bars and great stones, and even with cannon. The *Thomas* was dismasted and its hull stove in, and the King escaped by grappling onto a galley and taking it by storm. The Black Prince, too, lost his ship, and survived by capturing an enemy. The victory was won entirely by hand-to-hand fighting on deck; a number of Spanish ships, variously computed at fourteen to twenty-six, out of a fleet of forty, were taken, their crews being killed or thrown into the sea. This victory was even more popular in England than Crécy, especially in the southern counties, for the Castilians were a real threat to English prosperity. For the first time, Spanish naval power had been beaten in the open, and we are told that the Commons of England bestowed on Edward the title of 'King of the Sea'. It was his high noon.

5
The
Civilised
Warlord
1327-77

T HE KEY TO EDWARD III'S SUCCESS in imposing a remarkable stability on English political life during a period of war and rapid social and economic change lay, in the first instance, in his rich and contented family life. He was by no means faithful to his wife but they remained until the day of her death on remarkably close and affectionate terms. He was invariably generous to her, and included her in all his amusements and many of his adventures; she gave him unstinting loyalty. For reigning sovereigns, they spent an unusual amount of time in each other's company, and this closeness is reflected in Edward's building schemes for his palaces. Their mutual affection helps to explain why Edward never quarrelled with any of his numerous children. Philippa bore him twelve in all: seven sons, five daughters. Of these, three died in infancy or childhood, and his second daughter, Joan, was an early victim of the Black Death, dying at Bordeaux in 1348 while on her way to be betrothed to the eldest son of King Peter of Castile. Edward's touching letter to the bridegroom, announcing her death, has survived. 'With sighs, and sobs, and a heavy heart', he writes, he has to tell the Prince that, far from receiving an adopted son, as he had hoped, he has lost his daughter, 'in whom all the gifts of nature met, and whom also, because of the elegance of her manners, we sincerely loved beyond all our other children'.

The rest survived, and their marriages posed for Edward a variety of diplomatic and political problems. He was the first English king since Henry II with a large family to provide for. Disposing of the daughters was comparatively simple. Isabella, the eldest, he married to one of his leading French prisoners-of-war, Enguerrand de Coucy, whom he was anxious, for political reasons, to settle in England. He made him Earl of Bedford and a knight of the Garter, but the marriage was a failure, and de Coucy soon returned to France. Mary he married to Duke John IV of Brittany, to further his French dynastic policy, and Margaret to one of his generals, John Hastings, Earl of Pembroke, but both these girls died comparatively young.

Edward wished to make his sons leading territorial magnates, and buttresses of the throne; this was a risk that the father of a united family could take, though it was to pose serious problems for his successors. The Black Prince, as his heir, could be provided for out of the royal estates. He was made Earl of Chester

108

entieto wordant. er briant la
ces. Et quenouoie trop faisoiet
grant ioie er grant feste. apres

drap de soie batu aoz suo quatre
lances. et saichies tout ueraie
ement. que niu ne la ueist ql

LEFT The Pembridge Helm, which belonged to Sir Richard Pembridge, a famous captain in Edward's French wars.

OPPOSITE A fourteenth-century mêlée (Bodleian Add MS 2228 f 213). BELOW Geoffrey Luttrell receives a gilt helm from his wife, Agnes, and daughter-in-law, Beatrice Scrope.

at the age of three, and later Earl of Cornwall (raised to a duchy in 1337); the principality of Wales followed on his knighthood. The King's plans for the Black Prince's marriage were unsuccessful; in fact, he did not marry at all until he was thirty, when he made a love-match with Joan, the recently widowed Countess of Salisbury. Joan, daughter of an earl of Kent, was the leading beauty of her day – Edward had his eye on her himself, as we shall see – but she had little to give beyond her looks and keen intelligence. Moreover, the Prince seems to have married her without seeking the King's permission; it says a lot for Edward's forebearance that he not only raised no protest but, the next year, made the Prince Duke of Aquitaine and endowed him with his French possessions; at Bordeaux the Prince and his wife kept a Court which exceeded the King's own in brilliance.

Edward made his second surviving son, Lionel, Duke of Clarence, and found him two well-endowed brides. His first, Elizabeth, was the only child of the de Burgh Earl of Ulster, and through her Lionel became the leading Irish landowner, controlling the great Clare inheritance in Ulster and Connaught. This fitted well into Edward's scheme of government, for he was unable to visit Ireland himself, and his son became, in effect, his viceroy. On Elizabeth's death, Lionel was married to Violante Visconti, an heiress in the leading family of Milan, whose father was willing to pay two million gold florins, plus towns and castles in Piedmont, for the privilege. Lionel died shortly afterwards, but Edward had already arranged for his child, Philippa, to marry the Mortimer Earl of March, thus tying an important segment of baronial power to the Crown.

His fourth son, John, born at Ghent in 1340, was married by Edward to Blanche, younger of the Lancaster heiresses; in quick succession both John's father-in-law and his sister-in-law died, so John of Gaunt, as he was known, acquired the largest group of territories in England, next to the Crown itself – the duchy of Lancaster, and the earldoms of Leicester, Lincoln and Derby. It was for Blanche that Chaucer wrote his earliest Court work, *The Book of the Duchess*; but she died young, and Gaunt married Constance, co-heiress of Peter of Castile and Leon, thus becoming, as well as the richest man in England, an international figure of some consequence. Edmund of Langley, the fifth son, was married to Constance's sister, thus further strengthening the English party in Spain; and the youngest, Thomas of Woodstock, was comfortably placed with the co-heiress of the Bohun earls of Hereford, Essex and Northampton. All in all, Edward's marriage policy was a distinct success, neatly balancing foreign and domestic requirements.

Radiating from the royal family – and, as we have seen, intimately linked to it by arranged marriages – were the higher echelons of the nobility. Edward had judiciously reunited the magnates around the throne immediately on his assumption of power; but friendships, as Dr Johnson remarked, must be 'kept in constant repair', and this remained the King's policy. The man closest to him was Henry of Grosmont, the most powerful of them all, and after 1345 Earl of Lancaster. He fought along-side the King in the early Scottish campaigns, at Sluys and Winchelsea and at the siege of Calais; he held many independent commands in Gascony, Brittany and Normandy, and he was with the King on his last expedition in 1359. Henry was also used as a diplomat, and was in fact negotiating peace with France when he died. Edward believed in strengthening those he trusted: thus Henry was given the town of Bergerac, from the profits of which he built the splendid Savoy Palace in London, and in 1351 he was made the first non-royal duke, with his county raised to a palatinate – of course by then Edward already saw him as a future in-law, whose wealth and power would devolve on the royal family. Edward also rebuilt the Mortimer inheritance: he knighted the young heir, Roger, at the same time as the Black Prince (they were exact contemporaries), gave him a Garter and, in 1348, a barony; in 1354 the King arranged for Parliament to reverse the judgment on his grandfather, and Mortimer got back all the family estates and titles, including the earldom of March. Edward, indeed, actively intervened in the courts to hasten this process; but, then again, he arranged for the Mortimer heir to marry into the royal family. March, like Lancaster, was with the King on his last campaign.

Another close companion of Edward was the Fitzalan Earl of Arundel and Surrey, who commanded a squadron at Sluys and, with Northampton, the second division at Crécy. He fought, too, at Winchelsea, and the King steadily advanced his fortunes.

He was known as 'Copped Hat'. Most of the rest of Edward's friends – who also composed the bulk of his Council – came from the great nobility, fought with him in battle, and were advanced to earldoms: the Bohun brothers, earls of Hereford and Northampton, Beauchamp of Warwick, de Vere of Oxford, Ufford of Suffolk, Hastings of Pembroke and Ralph, Earl of Stafford. These were men of intelligence as well as military skill: Edward chose them for their education and character. Henry of Lancaster, indeed, was an author – of a devotional work which survives to puzzle us with its blend of naïveté and sophistication. Some of these magnates possessed considerable libraries. They were in every way well suited to share with Edward the business of government, and this circle of friendships, formed by policy, sealed on the battlefield and in the council chamber, and underpinned by marriage, constituted the bedrock of Edwardian stability. In such an atmosphere, treason became almost a forgotten word, and Edward was able to give it, for the first time, strict statutory definition, anchoring it firmly in the concept of allegiance to the royal person, and providing for those charged something approaching a fair trial. Edward seems consciously to have promoted the ties between monarch and aristocrat: thus, for the first time, he issued individual writs of summons to Parliament, and the House of Lords took shape not as the organ of a caste, but as the meeting-place of the heads of great families, there by virtue of their real power.

Edward did not, of course, hesitate to advance new men: he was always a realist. But the social style he generated made the going hard. Michael de la Pole, a Hull merchant who performed valuable financial jobs for the Crown, and served successfully at sea, got no more than a knighthood. The main road to social preferment was warfare, the only one older nobility accepted. Edward awarded barely enough titles of honour to balance casualties, and this shrewd policy aroused some grumbling (the same charge was made, equally foolishly, against his great successor Elizabeth I). What is more, he tightened up and systematised the heraldic system under which a man's status was formalised. The heralds adjudicated on claims to arms – that is, the right to wear coat-armour, proof of noble or gentle birth – and rival claims were settled by the King himself, presiding, with his constable and marshal, at a court of chivalry. Edward was no Justinian like his grandfather, but he frequently took personal charge of lawsuits involving two or more of his magnates. Thus, when Lady Wake brought a suit against the Bishop of Ely before Parliament in 1355, he promptly intervened: '*Jeo prenk la querele en ma main*' ('I take the quarrel into my hand').

Where many could, and did, rise rapidly was through the Church. Edward spent a great deal of time and trouble over ecclesiastical appointments; indeed, he had no choice, at a time when papal claims were being pushed vigorously, and when a loyal and able episcopate was essential to the smooth running of the realm. A medieval king could always come to grief over the Church. Edward, in practice, had to maintain a bench of bishops in which good administrators balanced men of piety, and papal nominees. He quickly abandoned his youthful attempt to staff the offices of state with laymen, who had to be paid in cash and lands instead of benefices. The men who ran the details of government – Offord, Dean of Lincoln, Thorseby, Bishop of Worcester, Edington of Winchester, Langham of Canterbury, and last but not least Wykeham of Winchester, all began as clerks in the royal service, and rose to be great men and loyal servants. Some became close personal friends of the King, who had a taste for the cloth as well as the brass. Thomas de la Mare, Abbot of St Albans, the greatest Benedictine of his day, was an intimate of Edward's, and godfather to his son Edmund, while William Clown, Augustinian Abbot of Leicester, was the King's favourite hunting companion (and also the model for Chaucer's sporting monk). Edward visited him in what is now the Quorn country almost every year, as we know from one of Clown's canons, the chronicler Henry Knighton. He maintained the finest pack of greyhounds, for harrying, in England and, when criticised, replied suavely that it was the duty of an abbot to his house to keep in with the great. These ecclesiastical friendships served Edward well in his relations with the Papacy, and evoked little comment; even his most formidable Pygmalion, Wykeham, was never attacked on personal grounds. But new laymen who aspired to the royal circle sometimes evoked sneers. Froissart noted that Sir Robert Salle was not of gentle birth, though he admitted his courage; Knighton

The Powell Roll of Armes, 1345–51, the most important heraldic record of Edward's reign. Each shield has the name of its bearer written in contemporary hand.

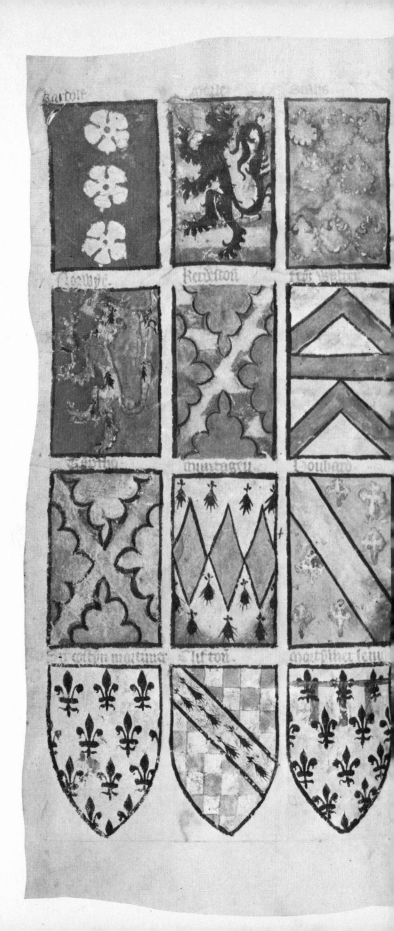

Sureton vfford.   Denbale.   Sir Edmund vfford.

Ingle.   Caulton.   Ingle le vucite.

Abbington.   Sibbigge.   Limerick.

[illegible]   furnehya   Iohan fiz will

complained about the exotic clothes of the new rich blurring social distinctions; and Walsingham thought that de la Pole was 'a man more suited to trade than knighthood, for he has spent his life as a moneylender not a soldier'. Edward took no notice. He needed to patronise money-men as well as up-and-coming captains; and he was sufficiently secure in his own regality and his military reputation to pick his friends as he thought fit. Thus, he was not ashamed to visit the rich Sir John Pulteney, four times Lord Mayor of London, at both his fine London houses and his new palace, Penshurst, in Kent – or, for that matter, to borrow large sums of money from him.

Edward's relations with his leading subjects, new and old, were enacted on the splendid stage of his Court. Indeed, he was the first English king to maintain an elaborate royal Court, which embodied his concept of the civilised warrior. His grandfather's Court had been a functional affair: part military camp, part centre of justice and administration. That of his grandson, Richard II, was to introduce rigid etiquette, and cut itself off, fatally, from its business and military origins. Edward III steered a balanced middle course, the arts functioning in harmony with the military virtues. It was typical of him that his Court orchestra – five trumpeters, one citoler (guitar), five pipers, one tabouretter, two clarion-players, one neckener (kettle-drum), one fiddler and three waits, or singers – became a military band in wartime, when its rates of pay were raised from $7\frac{1}{2}$d to a shilling a day; it was this band which played noisily when Edward entered Calais in triumph.

The civilised tone of the Court was set by Philippa, who brought from Flanders new standards and levels of sophistication. She not only introduced foreign poets and writers like Froissart but patronised Englishmen of the younger, better-educated generation, such as Chaucer. Nor did she commit the fatal error of earlier foreign queens, and surround herself with aliens; if she gilded her household with Continental talent, its basis was solidly English. She also introduced a marked feminine note – something which the Courts of Edward I and II conspicuously lacked, though for different reasons. Women attended the regular Court feasts in considerable numbers; they had a prescribed place in the ritual of tournaments – they were even accused of dressing up as men and taking part in them –

OPPOSITE A queen with her ladies, from an Arthurian romance written during Edward's reign. The popularity of the legend of Arthur led to the 'round table' tournaments and eventually to the founding of the Order of the Garter.

and they gave a fillip to the Court masques and 'disguisings'
which were just beginning to emerge, blending ancient religious
playlets into what was to become the English secular theatre.
Edward spent considerable sums of money on theatrical clothes
and props for these events. He liked lively evenings, with his
friends providing the entertainment. One of the reasons why
he married his daughter to de Coucy was that the Frenchman
had a fine singing-voice. He often danced himself: we have a
picture of him cavorting at Guildford over Christmas, wearing
'a harness of white buckram inlaid with silver', and his personal
motto: 'Hay, hay, the White Swan, by God's soul I am thy man.'

But of course the character of the Court was essentially
military. Its ritual revolved around tournaments. They were
no longer fought as mêlées in open fields, as in the thirteenth
century, but in lists, and they were already acquiring the
formality they retained until the Civil War ended jousting in

119

Rattent sur latenue de   trauitie sur les lices

Spectators watch with
concern as a knight is
knocked from his horse.

120

the 1640s. But they were nonetheless risky. Edward's dearest friend, William Montague, Earl of Salisbury – his chief companion in the 1330 *coup* – was killed at one in 1344. Heavy falls were frequent, and it may be that Edward's dotage was induced by reckless indulgence in this sport (which later ruined the health of Henry VIII). The chief tournaments were usually held to mark the great Church feasts of Christmas, Easter and Whitsun, but Edward showed an early tendency to increase their frequency. He seems to have acquired his taste for jousting as a very young man, under the auspices of Mortimer, who is reported to have held a 'round table' tournament as early as 1327. These Round Tables had a multiple political and social purpose. By re-enacting the story of King Arthur and his knights, they emphasised the ancient origins of the monarchy, with its claims not merely to British status, that is rule over all the British Isles, but to imperial sovereignty, for it was generally held that Arthur had broken away from the Roman Empire to assert the absolute independence of the kingdom. Arthur had been seized upon by the early Norman kings and their chroniclers to establish continuity of their rule with the pre-Saxon past; his myth-cycle, accepted as historical fact, had been an English cultural export from the last decades of the eleventh century, and Arthurian images – statues, wall-paintings, carvings – were now to be found all over west, central and southern Europe, and even in the Near East, where they had followed in the wake of the crusaders. The cult of Arthur was an important instrument in underwriting England's reputation as a leading military power and Edward's personal prestige as the reigning champion of chivalry. But, not content with Arthur, he successfully established St George – hitherto regarded as a patron of knights all over Christendom – as a peculiarly English possession. These symbols thus became part of Edward's incessant international propaganda in support of his French claims.

But, equally, the Round Table had a social purpose in strengthening the unity of England's military ruling class, grouped around the monarch. Confident, like Arthur, in his pre-eminence as a warrior and a knight, Edward could afford to have himself regarded, in the context of chivalry, as a first among equals, the equality being symbolised by the round

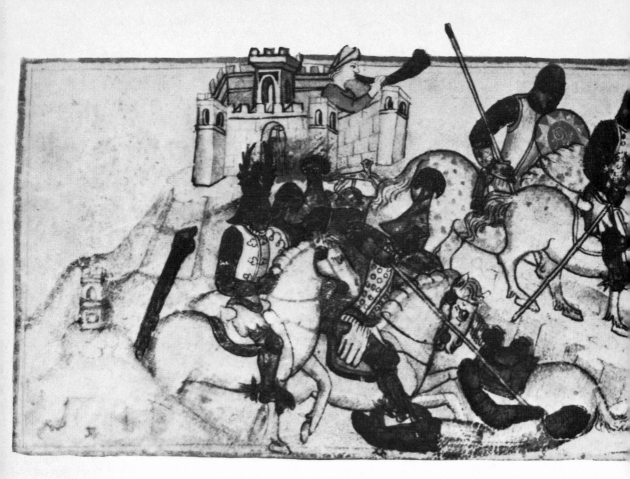

table, in the shape of a hollow circle, around which he and his knights sat. The status of courtiers was determined to a great extent by their military reputation, reinforced by their skill at the joust. The emphasis at Edward's Court was on informality: 'franchyse', which showed itself through a spontaneous ease of manner, was considered a mark of good breeding. The tone was set by Edward himself, who possessed the rare capacity to put men of all degrees at their ease, without any sacrifice of his royal dignity, and by his son the Black Prince. The Chandos Herald, who wrote the life of the latter, says that when he entered Bordeaux in triumph after his Spanish campaign, he dismounted before he reached the city gates, and walked through the town holding hands with his wife and little son. He always thanked his attendants and knights *'moult humblement'*. Both he and his father were prepared to joust against all comers; the King would literally risk his neck against a poor knight, provided, of course, that the challenger's

A mêlée from a fourteenth-century history of King Arthur. Edward's knights tried to imitate the code of chivalry that had been handed down in Arthurian legends.

122

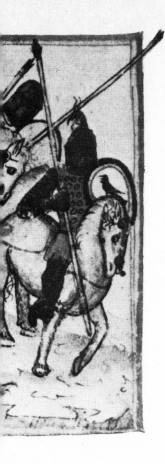

knightly status was authenticated. Within the circle of military power, there was a certain democracy.

The Edwardian tournament began to take shape after the Sluys victory. Edward held a large tournament at Windsor in January 1344, and the next month he formed a knightly association in Lincolnshire. At Windsor, in 1344, he held the first recorded Round Table of his reign; for the feast he wore a red velvet robe, 'furred and purpled'. The fur was ermine, ten furriers 'working with great haste upon the skins and furriery of the same robe'. Special tunics were made for 202 sergeants-at-arms and sixteen minstrels. But not until after his triumphant return from the Crécy campaign did Edward formalise the Round Table concept in the order, or society, of the Knights of the Garter. There has been much argument about its precise origin, as its early statutes are lost, surviving only in fifteenth-century transcriptions. But the main facts are now clear enough. Edward returned from France on 12 October 1347, and between then and the end of 1348 he held big tournaments at Windsor, Reading, Eltham, Canterbury, Bury and Lichfield. The first Garter ceremony was probably held on 24 June 1348 at Windsor, celebrating the purification of Philippa, on the feast of St John the Baptist, after the birth of her fourth son, William, in the castle. The story of the King picking up the garter, at a ball held at Calais to celebrate its fall, is first told by Polydore Vergil in the early sixteenth century, and was rejected by the great historian of the Order, Elias Ashmole. But it has an authentic ring, and the lady has been identified as the beautiful Joan of Kent, later to marry the Black Prince. It is quite possible that Edward used the words of the famous motto: at any rate, blue garters first appear in the Wardrobe accounts for this period: 'And for making a bed of blue taffeta for the King, powdered with garters, containing this motto, *Hony soit q. mal y. pense*' ('Evil to him who evil thinks').

Among the twenty-six founder knights of the 'society of the Garter', also called 'the fraternity of St George', were most of the King's chief friends and commanders: the Black Prince, Henry of Grosmont, the Earls of Warwick, Stafford and Salisbury, Roger Mortimer, Sir Bartholomew Burghersh, Sir Hugh Courtenay, Sir James Audley, Sir John Chandos and the Gascon Sir Jean de Grailly. The Queen and her ladies were made

'Dames of the Fraternity', and the knights were paralleled by a collegiate hospice to house twenty-six 'impoverished warriors'. The Garter knights were, in Ashmole's translation, all equal, 'to represent how they ought to be united in all Chances and various Turns of Fortune; copartners both in Peace and War, assistant to one another in all serious and dangerous exploits: and thro' the whole Course of their Lives to shew Fidelity and Friendliness one towards another'.

A tournament in France at St Inglevert.

The college itself, and the chapel of St George, was founded by letters patent issued on 6 August 1348, and endowed and regulated by a statute of 30 November 1352. This provided for a *custos*, later dean, twelve secular canons, thirteen priests or vicars, four clerks, six choristers and the twenty-six poor knights. To mark the importance of the foundation, Edward gave the college lands worth £655 15s a year, and granted it an extraordinary series of privileges and immunities. These are worth quoting in part, if only to show the burdens which might fall on land in the fourteenth century, representing the archaeological strata left by centuries of superimposed legal codes – the England of Edward III was already a society of great antiquity. Thus, the college was exempt from 'payment of toll, paviage, picage, barbicanage, terrage, pontage, murrage, passage, paiage, lestage, stallage, tallage, carriage, pesage, and from scot and geld, hidage, scutage, and working about castles, parks, bridges, and walls for the king's houses'. It was given the profits of a number of fines, a weekly market and two annual fairs; likewise, exemption was granted from 'gelds, dane-gelds, knight's fees and payments for murder and robbery ... ward-penny, aver-penny, tithing-penny, and hundred-penny, and discharged from grithbrech, forstall, homesoken, blod-wite, ward-wite, heng-wite, fight-wite, leyr-wite, lastage, pannage, assart and waste of the forest'. The college was to have its own stocks, pillory and tumbril for petty offenders, and to be allowed 'to erect gallows on their own soil, for execution of such malefactors as should fortune to be arrested within their jurisdiction'. As a final bonus, the corporation of Yarmouth were ordered by the King to send the collegians ten thousand red herrings a year, as punishment for murdering a magistrate.

To provide a splendid setting for the ceremonies at Windsor, Edward embarked upon the most extensive building pro-

124

The Order of the Garter
was founded in 1348. Its
founder members were the
King and the Black Prince
with twenty-four of their
chief knights. The
statutes emphasised the
equality of the members,
their co-operation in peace
and war and their
'Fidelity and
Friendliness' to each other.

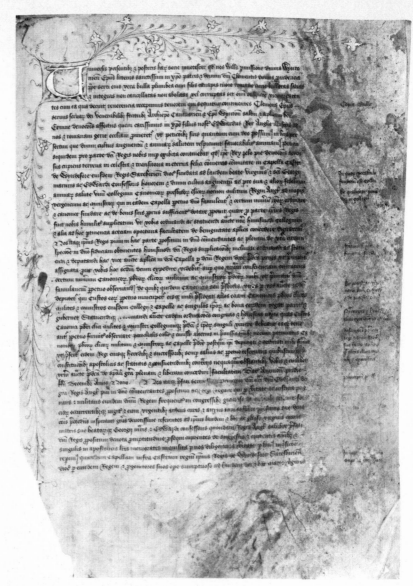

ABOVE A page from The Arundel White
Book c. 1430, the earliest surviving copy of
the statute book of the Order of the Garter.

LEFT Edward's two-handed sword, 6 feet
8 inches long, which hangs at Windsor.

OPPOSITE The entrance to the cloister of St
George, Windsor Castle, one of the earliest
Perpendicular buildings in England,
built in 1353.

126

gramme of his reign. He had always had particular affection for this castle, in which he was born; one of his first acts, on assuming royal authority in 1330, was to order costly repairs to it, and for most of his reign it was his chief residence, at which he received important embassies. As a pavilion for the round table itself, he turned to his master-carpenter, William Hurley, an architect of great imagination and an engineering genius. The pavilion has not survived, but we know what it looked like from Hurley's previous masterpiece at Ely Cathedral, on which it was based. At Ely, in 1322, the central tower, spanning the area where the main transept crosses the nave, had crashed down in total ruin, leaving a gaping hole in the heart of the church. The cathedral sacrist of the time, Alan of Walsingham, was a man of great energy and audacity. He persuaded the Court to lend him Hurley's services, and together they conceived and executed a wholly original plan. They opened up the space left by the collapsed tower into a huge octagon, seventy-four feet across, to form a vast amphitheatre for the choral services. They then threw up eight graceful groups of stone columns. It was impossible to cover such a wide space with stone, so the art of large-scale carpentry was invoked. The octagon was part-roofed by a timber vault, and this in turn was completed and crowned by a gigantic wooden lantern, held in place by the oblique timbers of the vaulting, with the ground ninety-three feet below it. This dramatic concept posed unique problems not merely in geometrical stress, the key to gothic architecture, but in sheer constructional engineering. The sixteen oblique struts, formed of single trunks of oak, rest at an angle on the eight stone columns and have to support a weight of four hundred tons of wood and lead. The lantern itself consists of a framework of eight oak trunks, each sixty-three feet long and a yard across. We do not know by what system of blocks and pulleys these massive weights were lifted nearly a hundred feet into the air and placed in positions where a mistake of a mere inch or two might bring the whole complex design crashing to the floor. But the octagon and lantern were successfully created – they are still there, 650 years later – and with this experience behind him, Hurley built Edward's pavilion in the 1340s.

Work continued at Windsor at a great pace during the 1350s

OPPOSITE The view up into the octagon of Ely Cathedral.

128

fic collato : memoria donatoris indelebi
liter perpetuetur. Et hoc tali largitate op
tinuit z condicione: ut de regno anglie ille
publice penitens pro execucione sibi tunc
de penitentie subirt exilium Redit oste
Celebrata igitur donacōe rex z fundat

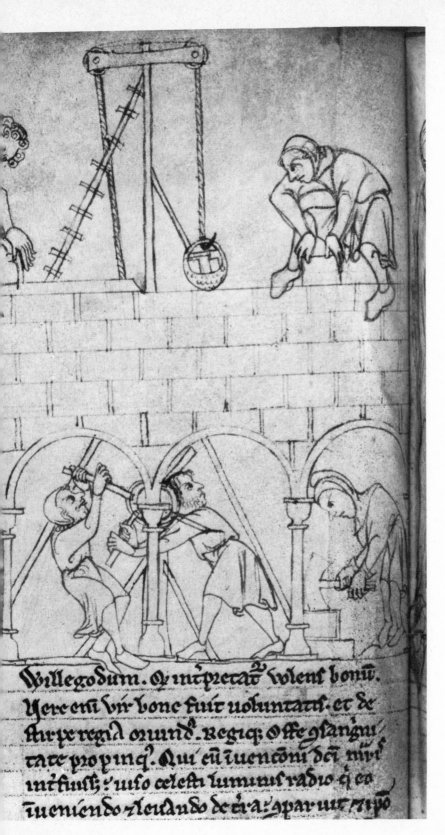

A king instructs his master builder.

and 1360s. The sixteenth-century antiquarian John Stow reported a tradition that it was at the suggestion of the Kings of Scotland and France, then held prisoners at the castle, that Edward embarked on a programme of enlargement. Or the spur may have been provided by the appointment of William of Wykeham, in 1356, as the surveyor of the castle and park. Wykeham was then thirty-two, and had long been in royal service there, first as keeper 'of the King's eight dogs at Windsor'. Wykeham was a practical polymath, with a wide range of skills, a great organising and financial official, a man who promoted his own ambitions by satisfying the King's taste for magnificence. At Windsor he developed the collegiate quadrilandriar structures which he was later to use, as Bishop of Winchester, for his own foundations at Winchester and New College, Oxford. The most intensive building period at Windsor was 1359–74; in the year 1363 alone, £3,802.17.8 was spent, over £900 on lead for roofing. For some years, annual expenditure was between £3,000 and £4,100. Craftsmen were subjected to impressment by the Crown, especially in the years of labour shortages which followed successive waves of the Black Death, but not even the King could get as many as he wished. Thus in 1360 sheriffs were ordered to supply 568 masons, but they never managed to get more than three hundred in any one year. Metal work was executed on the spot, the furnaces being fed by Newcastle coal. In 1367, for instance, a ship was chartered to carry coals – 726 chauldrons, or about eight hundred tons – at a total cost of £165.5.2, plus the hire of barges from London port to Windsor. Very little of Edward's work has survived, at least externally, but from later drawings we can gather that Edwardian Windsor presented a dramatic skyline, with a multitude of turrets and pinnacles.

Windsor was only one of a great series of royal residences, castles, manors, hunting-boxes and abbeys which Edward possessed, concentrated in the Thames Valley and its hinterland, but dotted all over England. We hear of him keeping Court at Berkhamsted and Eltham, Richmond, Henley, Gloucester and Reading, Woodstock, Marlborough, Guildford, King's Langley, Havering, Ottford and Leeds Castle, Kent. At many of these, extensive plans of reconstruction, or enlargement, were carried out, and there were new houses and foundations, notably the great chapel which Edward built and endowed at St Stephen's, Westminster, which soon became the permanent meeting-place of the House of Commons. Westminster in Edward's day consisted of the Great Palace, the Privy Palace and the Prince's Palace, all separate two-storey buildings; and huddled among them were lath-and-plaster tenements for the courtiers and officials, plus an occasional tall building like the White Hall. It probably looked a muddle from the outside – as it still did in the sixteenth and seventeenth centuries – but it was spectacularly rich and colourful within. A traveller had noted in 1322 that on its interior walls 'all the warlike scenes of the Bible are painted with marvellous skill'. This was the Painted Chamber of Henry III. But the Great Hall, the Little Hall, the Marculph Chamber and some of the smaller buildings were also covered with paintings. Under Edward III, a new Court art was beginning to emerge. He had the Great Chapter House adorned with God in Majesty, surrounded by Angels and Virtues; and in St Stephen's Chapel, he himself was portrayed with Philippa, surrounded by nine of their children, forty servers and thirty-six knights. It was destroyed by James Wyatt in 1800; but before then its appearance had been recorded in prose ('one universal blaze of splendour and magnificence ... a profusion of gilding and minute tracery and diaper') and drawings, from which modern reconstructions have been made. Edward also built a new decorated council room, the 'Chambre des Étoiles', or Star Chamber, in which the Council was beginning to sit as a judicial body; and at Windsor he had a painted chamber and the Rose Tower, decorated by William Burdon 1365–6, who used 67 lb of white lead, 12 lb of verdigris, 18 lb of red lead, 8 lb of vermilion, 7 lb of blue, and fourteen hundred leaves of gold. We know the names of over thirty painters who worked at Edward's expense.

These royal houses were ceasing to be fortifications – though they were still defensible – and were assuming the patterns of medieval Oxbridge colleges. At Eltham, Edward transformed a manor-house into a palace, spending £2,237 in the 1350s. Surrounded by a moat, and entered by the Great Bridge, it consisted of timber-framed buildings on stone foundations: both King and Queen had a Great Chamber, connected by a covered way; and there was a Great Hall and a Small Hall, a

133

garden and a vineyard. The King converted his house at Sheen, in Richmond, in a similar manner, spending over £2,000: here we see the emergence of the grand house, with multiple courts, large enough to accommodate a royal progress, which was to continue the pattern until the Civil War. These houses were rapidly acquiring plumbing systems and other amenities. In 1351 Robert Foundon was paid 56s. 8d for installing two large bronze keys, or taps, for the King's bath-tub at Westminster. In 1367 Edward added a bathhouse at Eltham, and in 1368–9 another, known as *'Les Stues'*, at Langley, with hot water piped direct into the tub. These bathrooms were paved with stone, and had an oven underneath; often there were tiles on the walls.

Personal latrines had not yet been designed in Edward's day (the water-closet itself emerged only in the late sixteenth century), but many new refinements were introduced at his Court. Edward appointed the first Court tapestry-maker, and he and his wife popularised pillows and blankets, feather-beds and sheets, silk coverlets and embroidered bed-curtains; none has survived, but we know that the King's friend Sir John Pulteney had bed-curtains patterned with lions' heads, eagles, *fleurs-de-lys*, violet popinjays, white roses, leaves, griffins and scenes from *Tristan*. It was left to Edward's grandson Richard II to introduce the pocket-handkerchief, and a variety of culinary refinements; but the Court cookery book, *The Forme of Cury*, compiled in his reign, reflected the style of eating already current at the end of Edward's life. This work, compiled 'with the assent and advysement of the maisters of phisik and philosophie' of the Court, lists 196 recipes. A typical *potage* was venison broth; one main dish was 'mawmenee', based on minced flesh of pheasant, mixed with sweet Greek wine, cinnamon, cloves and ginger, and two pounds of sugar; another was shelled oysters, cooked in wine with rice, ginger, sugar and mace, and a third deer's liver cooked in wine. Puddings, called 'sotiltees', were brightly decorated, a typical one being 'moree', or mulberries cooked with honey. Lombardy mustard was a favourite condiment, and olive oil was used instead of butter. Edward dined well, and he drank well, of fine claret. King John of France, no mean judge, was deeply impressed by the feasts at Windsor, most of all by the fact that the King was able to pay for them, not in gold or silver, but in

OPPOSITE A mason and carpenter at work.

135

mere wooden Exchequer tallies, a testimony to the renewed strength of English royal credit.

But if Edward's Court life reflects the international culture and luxury he acquired on his many Continental expeditions, the wars were also producing something radically different, and much more important, among the nation as a whole: a new, strident sense of English nationalism.

An English
embroidered cope of the
late fourteenth century.

137

6 A Nation

WHEN EDWARD III CAME TO THE THRONE, England was still a small country, by the standard of France, with a population of not much over three million. But population had been increasing fast, and it may be that by Edward's early years it had reached saturation point, at least in terms of existing agricultural techniques, and had begun to stabilise itself, before contracting sharply in the years following the Black Death. The famine years beginning in 1315 had brought a decisive check to the system of 'high farming' which had been such a striking feature of the thirteenth-century English economy. Under this, the great lay and ecclesiastical proprietors farmed many thousands of acres of their own demesnes themselves, producing cash-crops for sale and even export, enforcing the labour services of their bondsmen and maintaining large herds of cattle and enormous flocks of sheep – sometimes up to twenty thousand on certain rich abbeys and priories. After the famine years, high farming ceased to expand, and there was a growing tendency for big proprietors to dispose of outlying lands, and even whole manors, by sale or for cash rents on long leases. Thus more and more land was being independently worked, or owned, by medium-sized or small farmers, or even villeins. The concept of a privileged, French-speaking landed class, in exclusive possession of freehold property, was being eroded, as more men got what they felt to be a stake in their own country. Society was becoming far more complex, ownership of wealth more diffused, forms of economic activity more varied.

This England was still overwhelmingly agricultural in occupation and outlook, though the section of the economy producing food, skins and wool for sale, rather than for subsistence consumption, was growing at some speed. From poll-tax returns taken at the end of the reign, the most populous districts of the countryside appeared to be parts of Lincolnshire, with a density of up to fifty-four persons per square mile, Norfolk, with forty-eight, and parts of Leicestershire, Bedfordshire and Northamptonshire with forty – this compared to an overall average of about eight hundred for England and Wales today. Thus villages were small and sparse. But towns were growing, in size and numbers, and it was a matter of royal policy – for military as well as economic reasons – to promote their prosperity. The Crown also created

PREVIOUS PAGES A miller carries grain to the windmill, from the *Romance of Alexander* (MS Bodley 264 f 81).

OPPOSITE A mixed team of ox and ass drawing a plough, from the story of Cain and Abel in the Holkham Bible picture book of the mid-fourteenth century.

140

Saunt Cajrn de deur: estoit maudit. Den loſnz deſleuk ſi ſeufuiſt. E
terrat tere: ꝛ ſemoiſt ble. E ſileuk ꝯmaudꝑt. eſtre muee. ke deuz de ceel ne
oiꝉ pꝭ kuil E ke me out poi ne uertu. E de luſ euiꝉ un graunt pꝭgꝭ. E
muecs geuꝝ ꝛ tuces maudꝭ La luſtenaunce ꝗ creiꝉh ſur tere: nuſl de
eus ne la uouliſt crere. ke deuz co ouꝉ eſte: coe dedzeſt duſt aeſtre loſſ ble.
Tuces eſtoſeiꝉ de male creaunce. Poꝛ ceo auꝭn lui urꝉ meſchaunce. E a ꝉꝉ
ſꝓ numeineiꝉ. Apꝛes uerrez la gſe coment. ke ſke ſeiꝉ de deuz maiſꝺꝉ
cueſchaunꝉ aꝝ ſaunꝝ reſpꝑꝉ. Enter ſuꝝ de erutage Cajrn ꝛ fut. ſouli image.
E treuz ceuſ ꝗ treſon ſuiꝉ. Touꝝ enſemble en enfer uoiꝉ.

new towns, such as Edward I's port of Winchelsea and his garrison towns at Caernarvon, Conway and Beaumaris, and Edward III's own fortress-port at Queenborough, called after Philippa. Edward III took positive steps to prevent the 'decay' of established towns, notably at Newcastle in 1357 and Lincoln in 1365. But his chief attention was focussed on London, whose vitality he underpinned by stabilising his courts and government at Westminster, his chief mint and armoury at the Tower, and his vast Wardrobe at Baynard's Castle below Fleet Street. During his reign, the city became a true capital, both economically and politically, comparable to the other great cities of northern Europe. At his death, poll-tax returns show its population to have been 34,971; York was 10,872, Bristol 9,518, Plymouth 7,256, Coventry 7,226. No other town reached 6,000. The growth of city life, and of urban privileges, and the increasing part which burgesses played in the government of the country through Parliament all contributed to the spread of a national consciousness. More and more people were thinking less in terms of their village, manor or great estate on which they lived, and more in terms of the community as a whole – of England.

Government, too, was beginning to adopt a national perspective. It was much better informed than its predecessors, as the growing speed of travel eroded distances and made it possible to plan administrative acts on the basis of reasonably up-to-date information. The Gough Map in the Bodleian Library, Oxford, evidently compiled shortly before 1360, shows a network of roads which approximates to the system which existed in the seventeenth century. Surfaces were improving, allowing carts to transport heavy goods long distances inland. As government became more dependent on revenue raised from taxation, so it sought to strengthen those sectors of the economy from which taxes were raised: its aims were practical rather than altruistic, but the effect of its efforts was to raise output and thus to allow men to see the connection between government policy and their own prosperity – to relate themselves to a national context. Thus, Edward pushed the development of the Cornish tin industry, which eventually brought the Crown over £2,000 a year in revenue through the stannaries of the duchy of Cornwall. He encouraged the mining

PREVIOUS PAGES Southern England from the Gough Map of *c.* 1360 showing the Tower of London and the major towns, castles and cathedrals.

of coal wherever it could be found, but especially in the big Newcastle field, which by the end of his reign was exporting over seven thousand tons a year. When he gave his protection to the Gateshead miners in 1368, he said that he wanted coal to be taken to all parts of the kingdom. Iron-working, too, got his support, for economic as well as military reasons.

Edward devoted more attention to the wool and cloth industry than to any other aspect of economic policy – not surprisingly, for it was the chief form of taxable wealth. The politics and economics of wool were complex and Edward and his advisers never completely mastered them. Government policy oscillated violently, in response to international factors and domestic pressures, and the whole problem cost the King much angry heartache: more than once he indicated his anxiety to free the Exchequer from its heavy dependence on wool; but this was impossible. His object was to adopt a system which made tax-collecting easy and efficient without depressing the trade. Wool exports came from many parts of the country, chiefly the South Downs, the Midlands, East Anglia and Yorkshire; the best quality from the Severn Valley, the Cotswolds, Leicestershire and Lincolnshire. To strengthen his financial position on the eve of war, Edward adopted in 1337 a staple system which obliged growers to channel their products through a central depot. He placed it first at Antwerp, then at Bruges. With a staple, as opposed to a free system dispersed over many centres, Edward could control and tax the trade more easily; better still, he could raise money from bankers and big merchants in exchange for tax-farms. But a staple tended to inhibit growth, and it favoured a few big monopolists at the expense of the small men. In 1353 the Ordinance of the Staple replaced a foreign centre with fifteen staple towns in England, Wales and Ireland, and this was confirmed by statute two years later. But it left alien middlemen in charge of export operations, and in 1360 the Commons petitioned for free trade; Edward replied that he could not afford it. In 1363 he switched again, consolidating the staple in Calais, under a quasi-monopoly system. This gradually became more popular, not least because any permanent system was preferable to frequent changes of policy.

Where Edward was more consistent, and successful, was in

promoting the growth of an English cloth trade, and thus helping to change the country from a primary producer into a large-scale manufacturer. He was aided by technical developments which made it possible to switch from manpower to water-power in the process of fulling, and thus to move the fulling process from towns to rural areas where the wool was grown. Edward brought a good many Flemish cloth-workers to England and Wales, and gave them his protection against local xenophobia. Once cloth was produced in quantity, it

147

could be taxed; but here again Edward had to steer a careful middle course between the need for revenue and the need to keep the competitive edge of English cloth exports.

Checking weights and measures in a market.

All these economic problems necessarily meant continuous and detailed consultation with the interests involved, through the forum of Parliament. It was the demands of economic policy, no less than the war itself, which brought the Crown closer to the people, and so helped to bind a nation together. Yet the war, above all, gave the process an emotional intensity no other force could have supplied. In a sense, the war was very popular indeed. Froissart, a friendly but critical observer, noted:

> The English will never love and honour their king unless he be victorious and a lover of arms and war against their neighbours and especially against such as are greater and richer than themselves. Their land is fuller of riches and of goods when they are at war than in peacetime. They take delight and solace in battles and slaughter; they covet and envy other men's wealth beyond measure.

But he also points out: 'The King of England must needs obey his people, and do all their will.' This was an exaggeration, but it grasped the point that, for the English, war was a collective effort, and to some extent a collective responsibility. Edward's army was national – there was no lack of volunteers, as we have

seen. The extent of national involvement is shown, for instance, by a roll of 1355: in seventeen Derbyshire manors, more than half the fighting men were actually on campaign. Hence, Edward was always anxious to show that the war was the business of the people, as well as the pursuit of his own personal claim. To keep the public informed, official news of the war was sent to sheriffs in the form of letters, for reading at shire courts and other centres where men congregated. Equally important was Edward's use of the clerical system of communication. Instructions for patriotic prayers, or ceremonies of thanksgiving, were sent to the archbishops, who passed them on to the bishops, and so, through the archdeacons, to the parish clergy. The parish church on Sunday became the great organ of royal propaganda, its triumphant peal of bells the bucolic herald of victory.

But Parliament, above all, was the national theatre on which the war-effort was discussed and promoted. To its members, Edward presented the war as a putative joint-stock enterprise, conducted with their advice and consent, and in their interests as well as his own. When abroad, he would send distinguished field commanders, such as Sir Walter Manny, to report the news in detail. Sometimes he spoke himself. His ministers read official dispatches of victories, asked for advice about embassies and negotiations or, for instance, gave the text of the French plan to invade England which had been captured at Caen. In 1351 Edward instructed his Chancellor to tell both Houses, in his opening address, that they had been summoned because the King wished to satisfy all the grievances of his people. He thanked the magnates and the Commons for the great love they had always shown him, for the large aids and subsidies they had granted him and for all that they had suffered, in both body and goods, for the maintenance of the war and the defence of the realm. In return, he would do all in his power for their 'ease, comfort and favour'. Nearly two and a half centuries later, Elizabeth I would be speaking in similar terms during the great war with Spain. The Parliament Rolls show that the King accorded Parliament a constitutional place in the actual decision-making. In April 1354 it was presented with a draft of the proposed Treaty of Guines, and asked if its members wanted the King to secure a perpetual peace with France: they replied, according to the record, *'entierement et uniement'* – 'Yes, Yes!' The Treaty of Calais of 1360 was formally ratified by Parliament, and three years later there was an attempt to present a national balance sheet.

One reason why Edward – like other wise sovereigns – was always anxious to meet Parliament more than halfway, and to concede freely what might otherwise be extracted under duress, was that he wanted to avoid any formalisation of his relations with Parliament, which could only be to his disadvantage. Courtesy and conciliation were a cheap price to pay to avoid definition. His personal rule began against a political background in which Parliament was being forced, almost against its will, to fill the vacuum of power left by the incompetence of his father. And this inevitably led men to think out clearly, and set down in words, constitutional propositions which had hitherto been left conveniently vague. Thus, in the early 1320s, an experienced Parliamentary official had written and circulated a document known as the *Modus Tenendi Parliamentum* – The Way Parliament Should be Held – the first attempt to describe the theory and practice of Parliamentary government, and the distant ancestor of Eskine May. This was more a political manifesto than an account of what actually happened, but it showed the way men's minds were moving. It presents the King not as a sovereign dealing with an advisory body, but as a member of that body, subject to its rules and procedures. Thus, the King is to sit in the middle of the 'side of honour', or the Great Bench, and must be present for the first time on the sixth day of the session. He hears the sermon, then the address by the Chancellor (or the senior judge), given standing. '… Members of Parliament, no matter who they are, except the King, will stand while speaking, so that all members may hear them.' Then the King speaks, seated. The *Modus* goes on: 'The King is required to be personally present without fail in parliament, unless he is prevented by bodily illness.' In that case he can keep to his room, provided that it is not outside the manor or town where Parliament is sitting; moreover, twelve magnates and worthies had to visit him and witness his state of health, and receive his commission: 'The reason for this provision is that there used to be outcry and murmuring in parliament about the absence of the King, because it is …

dangerous to the whole community of parliament and the kingdom when the king is absent ... nor should he nor may he absent himself except in the aforesaid circumstances.' The King was to be present each day, when Parliament met, at 6.30, or half an hour after sunrise in winter. Parliament was to be held in a public place, and not in 'a secret or private place', and the doors must be open, though guarded. Finally: 'The King is the head, the beginning and the end of parliament ... for this reason, the King alone comprises the first rank.'

This attempt to reduce the King to a mere functional official – though an honoured one – of the system was not compatible with the realities of fourteenth-century power-politics and administration. Nevertheless, it was equally clear that Parliament, including the Commons, had ceased to be an optional element in the way the country was run, and during Edward's reign practice came steadily closer to the procedures laid down in the *Modus*. The Commons were absent from only four of the twenty-five Parliaments held in the decade 1327–37, and by the end of the reign their presence was, in effect, mandatory. Moreover, the frequency with which Edward held Parliaments – nearly one a year – indicates that he regarded it as part of the regular process of government. There was also a steady movement to consolidate and regularise – though not to define in words – its powers. By the 1350s Edward had accepted that an ordinance passed by him and his Council must, on matters of importance, be subsequently ratified by Parliamentary statute; and the courts came to recognise that a statute overrode any other source of law. Parliament's financial powers, too, expanded. Thus, from the start, Edward agreed that the consent of the knights and burgesses was necessary for any tax on movable goods (the traditional tenths and fifteenths), since it was clearly levied by shire and borough. He argued, on the other hand, that this did not apply to levies on wool, or customs duties, which were imposed at the ports. The Commons answer was that he had, indeed, an 'ancient right' to charge half a mark (6s. 8d) for every sack of wool and every three hundred woolfelts exported, but that *maltotes*, or additional duties, could be imposed only by consent. This Edward felt obliged to concede in 1362. Moreover, the Commons were increasingly insistent that the money be well spent. In 1340 they asked for an audit of tax-accounts; in 1353 they appropriated a wool tax to the sole purpose of conducting the war; and by the end of the reign, as we shall see, they were going much further in demanding a voice in the spending, as opposed to the mere raising, of money.

The nation was flexing its muscles in other ways, and not necessarily through the Parliamentary process. If the 'political nation' made its weight felt, might not the 'real nation' do likewise? The composition of Parliament was still imperfectly defined; but it was already confined essentially to the landed and propertied classes. What of those beyond, trained to arms and, in large numbers, increasingly experienced in their use?

The real nation was brought into play by an event which did, indeed, serve as a reminder that all men were equal, or at least mortal. The Black Death probably originated during the winter of 1338–9 in central Asia, near Lake Issy-Koul in Semiriechinsk, a region in which bubonic plague was, and still is, endemic. It spread east to China, south to India and west to the Crimea, which it reached eight years later. By October 1347 it was in Sicily, whence it spread, by galley, to Genoa and Venice, southern Italy, North Africa and Spain. By August 1348 it was at Bordeaux, where it killed the little Princess Joan, and it reached the English ports at the same time as the news of her death. By January 1349 it was raging fiercely enough for Edward to prorogue Parliament on the grounds that it was unsafe to come to London.

The plague was a combination. Its chief element was the bacillus *Pasteurella Pestis*, carried by fleas in the hairs of rodents, notably the tough and active black rat. The symptoms were swollen and enflamed glands, particularly in the groin, armpit and neck, and subcutaneous haemorrhage – hence the 'black' appearance – accompanied by intense pain and apparent madness. There was a more lethal variant, of pneumonic or pulmonary plague; and a third, equally lethal, of septicaemic plague, spread by human fleas. The first variety could kill in four to seven days; the latter two in two days or less. These combinations of plague arrived three times in Edward's reign (1348–9, 1361–2, 1369), the second outbreak striking with particular ferocity at children, and thus affecting the labour market in his last decade. The net effect was to reduce the population by roughly one third, though the incidence varied

A German
plague cross of the
fourteenth century.

enormously from one district or even village to another.

Seen from one angle, the economic effect of the plague was beneficial: it produced that radical cut in population which modern geo-politicians are trying to bring about by the much slower methods of mass birth-control, and with the object of raising living standards. There can be no doubt that, at least in England, people lived better in consequence. Wages on the vast Winchester estates rose sixty per cent from the decade 1320–9 to the decade 1370–9; on the Westminster estates, during the same period, by nearly a hundred per cent. At the same time, grain prices fell, so that real wages were very much higher at the end of Edward's reign than at the beginning. This is reflected, too, in the attempts of big estates to raise productivity by introducing labour-saving devices like the butter-churn, and replacing the sickle by the scythe. In one sense, plague benefited the higher classes, too. Death led to rapid promotion among the clergy, to the amalgamation of lay estates big and small, and to a consequent rise in disposable incomes among the well-to-do and rich – reflected in their sumptuous buildings and the spread of luxury habits. The first and spectacular phase of the Black Death brought only a short pause in Edward's military operations, or for that matter in his building activities; it may even have brought actual benefit to his Exchequer. It certainly stimulated the building of new colleges: Trinity Hall, Gonville Hall and Corpus Christi at Cambridge, New College at Oxford. Merton was able to buy land cheap, and so expand; New College may have been built on the site of Oxford's largest plague-pit, a curious piece of symbolism

Yet on the other hand, the cataclysm shook traditional social relationships, which were already under pressure from other forces, in a way which men could see and feel – and resent – in their daily lives. Well-fed clerical chroniclers, and Parliament-arians who had survived and profited, were bitterly and vocally aware of ocular evidence that class distinctions were dissolving as inferior men profited from the shortage of labour and aped the dress and habits of their betters: hence the repeated and largely ineffective efforts of Parliament to impose sumptuary legislation, to restore, as it were, the ancient mould, at least in outward appearance. The King and Parliament were also concerned by other phenomena: notably the evidence of

depopulation. The Black Death does not seem to have extinguished many villages at a stroke, but it weakened a good many more, especially in areas of low agricultural productivity, and so low wages, rents and returns. Landowners contracted their operations, tenant farmers moved, followed by labourers in search of higher wages. The result was reflected in the tax-records: sometimes the sheriffs and other collectors were obliged to file nil-returns – there were no tax-payers left. Government acted, first by ordinance, then in the Statute of Labourers (1351) to halt these irresistible forces. It tried to control wages, prices and the movement of labour, something beyond the capacity of any modern government, let alone a medieval one. Initially, it had the backing of the entrenched classes, appalled by the rise in wages and conscious, for the first time, that they were at the mercy of men plying for hire in a seller's market. But the law could not be enforced. Bondsmen left their

A man with a scythe. As a result of the shortage of labour after the Black Death, the scythe replaced the less-efficient sickle.

155

villages to become wage-labourers, conscious that the prospect of affluence was well worth the small risk of recapture. In its anxiety to punish offenders, government enormously enlarged the powers of local, unpaid Justices of the Peace, who were given the duty of fixing wages and administering the 1351 statute, and from 1362 bidden to meet in plenary quarter sessions. But landowners and farmers could not afford to observe the statute; to stay in business they needed labour, and to get it they had to pay up, and thus evade the law. The net result of all these changes, and the effort to efface them, was to draw government and Parliament into ever-widening spheres of economic activity, to bring them into closer contact with the 'real nation', and thus to involve more and more people in the operations of the state.

There was a further factor making for the growth of national consciousness: the emergence, as it seemed, of a common enemy within, in the shape of the international Church. This was closely linked with the development of anti-French feeling. Under Clement V (1305–14), the Papacy had moved to Avignon, within the French sphere of influence. Not until after Edward's death did the great schism break out, and so enable both sides in the war to back rival pontiffs. But already by his early years, the Avignon Papacy was producing more and more specific disputes between the popes and English interests, and with the outbreak of war, the efforts of the Pope to promote peace – which, as we have seen, served French acquisitive aims – aroused hostility. The popes were neutral: but they seemed to be neutral for France. Moreover, it was generally believed that the revenues derived by the popes and other foreigners from English churches – the system known as papal provisions – were used, at least in part, to finance the King's enemies. In 1334 Edward first voiced this resentment in a strong letter; he made further protests in 1344 and 1348 and, these being unavailing, he caused Parliament, which was willing enough, to pass the statutes of Provisors (1351) and Praemunire (1353). These, as subsequently amended and strengthened, in theory reduced the power of the Papacy in England virtually to matters of doctrine. In practice, they gave Edward what he wanted: a large range of options, and great freedom of manœuvre, in dealing with Avignon. On the one hand, the King could represent himself

OPPOSITE ABOVE
Gravediggers from the
Romance of Alexander
(Bodleian Roll 79G f 69).
BELOW Death reaches for
a man with his flesh hook.
(Bodleian MS Douce 88.)

157

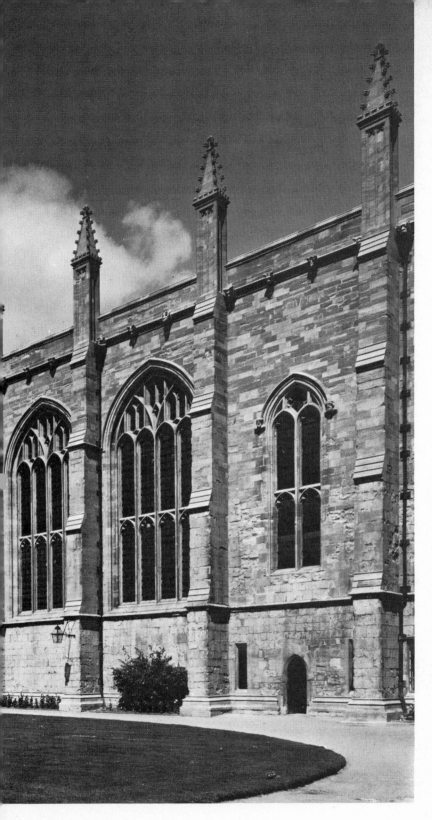

The front quad and chapel of New College, Oxford, founded by William of Wykeham, Bishop of Winchester, in 1379. Having been formerly a Surveyor of the King's Works, Wykeham took great interest in the college buildings which were arranged in a quadrangle, the hall and chapel opposite the scholars' rooms and the entrance tower and the muniment tower facing each other. This set a pattern for future colleges.

159

as the helpless agent of Parliament, tied hand and foot by statute and forced to act against the Pope's wishes and his own. On the other, he could consent to evade the statutes in return for a papal *quid pro quo*. This is what, in fact, usually happened. The system of financial relationships between the Pope and the English Church was vulnerable to royal intervention, made possible by the statutes, at the expense of both parties. Thus, when the Pope wanted to tax the English clergy, Edward was certain to demand, and get, his cut. In any event, the wars made it difficult to transfer money abroad. In 1360 the Pope demanded a subsidy from the English Church for the bizarre purpose of contributing to the ransom of King John of France; Edward allowed this, to the extent of £30,000, since it went straight into his own pocket. On the other hand, when the Pope, retaliating for the second Statute of Praemunire (1365), demanded a renewal of Peter's Pence, Edward simply referred the request to Parliament, where the Lords promptly pronounced it illegal and unconstitutional.

Edward succeeded in taxing the clergy heavily himself, by means of tenths, each of which raised some £20,000. He did not always get his own way, and in particular he failed to integrate the provincial convocations of the clergy with Parliament. But as a rule he could rely on the solid support of the bench of bishops, most of whom were his personal appointments, drawn from the royal bureaucracy. Naturally, to secure papal approval for these appointments – always, in the end, forthcoming – he had to give the Pope something in return, usually in the form of benefices for papal nominees. To do this meant evading Provisors, and sometimes Parliament protested. But Edward could argue that he was, in fact, steadily diminishing the number of papal provisions, and usually, by a process of conciliation, he could get all parties to agree. It was the same with alien priories, that is, English offshoots of Continental mother-abbeys, whose inmates were widely regarded as spies. The Pope wanted the *status quo*; Parliament outright confiscation; Edward a middle course, under which he milked, or farmed, the priories, under threat of seizure, rather as his predecessors had farmed the Jews. All this took diplomacy, but the system held until Edward lost his grip, when Parliament toppled over into outright anti-clericalism. It was heading in

Gloucester Cathedral

The continual procession of pilgrims to revere the shrine of Edward II at Gloucester Cathedral brought so much revenue to the abbey church that a great reconstruction was undertaken in Perpendicular style.
RIGHT The stained glass rounded at the base of the Crécy window depicting a fourteenth-century golfer.
BELOW At the western end of the choir flying arches carry the springing of the last division of the choir vault.

RIGHT The presbytery with the great Crécy window which was commissioned by Lord Bradeston, a commander at the battle, as a memorial to the great victory.

this direction all the time, of course, for war fever inevitably led Englishmen to resent the manner in which their own clergymen were financially, doctrinally and organisationally subject to an alien institution on French territory. It was one more way in which they were beginning to see themselves as a nation apart, and the Channel as a frontier – plainly ordained by God rather than man – which conditioned all aspects of life.

It was certainly becoming a cultural frontier, in a number of striking ways. Hitherto England had taken her architectural styles, spectacularly embodied for all to see in her soaring cathedrals, at some remove, from France, and especially those territories controlled by the French king. The English had introduced significant local variations, springing from climate, native craftsmanship and the peculiar needs of their church. But the patterns were basically Continental in inspiration, and often applied by French master-builders, sometimes even in stone imported from Normandy. The growth of English national consciousness, and the development of native cultural resources, made some divergence inevitable; the Hundred Years' War undoubtedly speeded the process. England moved away from the flamboyant Gothic of the French fourteenth century – which, significantly, continued to be used in France's ally, Scotland – and produced the peculiarly English style we call Perpendicular. Its first great expression was in the rebuilding of Gloucester Abbey, made possible by the contributions to Edward II's shrine. There, in the decade 1330–40, the architect William de Ramsay refashioned the old Norman choir by constructing a perpendicular stone screen upon the inside surface of the arcade; he pulled down the roof of the choir and the east end, and then carried the screen walls, pierced by tall windows, up to a height of nearly a hundred feet, roofing it in with a great fretted vault. In place of the old apse, he put in a square east end to contain the largest painted window in the country. To make this huge glass wall secure, he had to get its end corners onto the old Norman foundations; so he canted the walls of the eastern end outwards to effect this alignment. It is a daring and perilous concept. The great glass wall, begun in 1347 and finished two years later, marked the high noon of Edward's reign. It was paid for by Lord Bradeston, who commanded the fifth part of the King's division at Crécy; he figures on the glass, together with the arms of his companion in battle, Sir Maurice Berkeley. It is still known as the Crécy Window, and rightly, for there can be little doubt that it was a memorial to the victory. So a triumph of English militarism was immortalised in a masterpiece produced by the first real frenzy of English nationalism.

The theme of patriotism appears again and again in the vast construction work which, scarcely interrupted by plague and war, was transforming England's cathedrals and public edifices during these times, at Westminster and York, at Exeter, Ely and Winchester. No trace, alas, remains of Edward's two personal foundations, the Cistercian St Mary's, Eastminster, and his nunnery at Dartford. But he himself appears in the windows of the Lady Chapel at York, between St Peter and Samuel, against a background powdered with Garters; and the image of his national patron and namesake, Edward the Confessor, figures in St Stephen's Chapel in Westminster, over the courts of the King's Bench and Common Pleas in the Hall, over the gate into Deans' Yard, on the back of the screen in St Edward's Chapel and again in a window on the south side of the Abbey. How many other artistic vindications of the national spirit – in glass and stone, in wood and alabaster, paint and ivory – have been lost we can never know. But artists and craftsmen, Church and State, combined to impress on Edward's people daily and ocular reminders of their new nationhood.

There were verbal reminders, too, of infinitely greater scope and importance. The wars completed the destruction of the French language in England, so that by the end of the century it had virtually passed out of use as the vernacular of government and the ruling class, lingering on in archaic forms only in the recesses of the law-courts and ancient Parliamentary ceremonial. Of course the mass of the people had never spoken French, except in the bureaucratic pidgin made necessary by their occasional brushes against the state. Even in the thirteenth century, some statutes had been written in English as well as French and Latin. By the mid-fourteenth century, popular pressure to demote French as the administrative tongue was becoming irresistible: paradoxically enough, it was the sheer conservatism of English officialdom which allowed it to linger on so long. The war was not the only factor in its decay. John

The Flowering of English Literature

The wars with France brought to an end the dominance of French as the language of government and literature. A new generation emerged who wrote poetry and prose in their native tongue. Chaucer (below) was the greatest of these although his most famous work, *The Canterbury Tales*, was not written until after Edward's death.

OPPOSITE A psalm from the earliest surviving Wyklif Bible of the late fourteenth century. Wyklif made the first complete translation of the Bible into English.
ABOVE A page from *Sir Gawayne and the Grene Knight*, an Arthurian romance in alliterative verse, written by an unknown author in Lancashire.

By þe tretynce of vnpitues Blyssful ys þ þat þe lyrcus vnkyn þ wette of propilete þo ot not gone i þe coūseil of vntrist ynoule: z i þe wete of synful stod not: i þe chayer of pestilence sat not. But i þe lawe of þe lord ys wol i þe lawe of hy he schal swetell þenken day z nyȝt. And he schal be as a tree þat plantid besides þe don renner of watr þat hys frute schal ȝyue i hys tyme. And þe lef of hy schal not fallen z alle thyng whit euer he schal don schulen wexen welle. Not so þe vnpitousl not so: But as pulde þat after prouny þe wynd fro þe face of þe erþ. Þerfore ryssen not þe vnpitouse i dome: hy þil ȝe couseil of ryȝtuse. Þory lord hath knowe þe wee of þe rytuise: z þe gynne of þe vnpitouse schal pischen.

Why sruckeden gentilis: z puplis swetely þorten inwardly wexne thing. Þer stoden nees þe kyngis of þe erþ: z princes camen togid i to can aȝeu þe lord z aȝeu hys arist. Gobreke wee þe bondis of hem z aser proune ȝee fro vs þe ȝok of hem. Þat dwelley i heuenes schal scorne hem: z þe lord schal bemourwe hem. Þane he schal speke to ȝe i hys wratthe: z i hys wod nesse disturben ȝe togid. I forsoy am sett kyng fro hy vp on euon þe holy mont of hy pischie hys heste. Þe lord seye to me my sone þu art: I to day gat þee. Aske of me z I schal ȝyue to þee gentilis þyn eritge: z þy possesou þe termes of þe erþ. Þou schalt goune ȝe i an yone ȝeȝer: z as a vessel of a poreter breke ȝe togid. And nowȝ kyngis vnderstondey: bey tauȝt þat dome þe erþ. Serueȝ to þe lord i drede: z ful out glaḍeȝ to hy wt tremblyng. Galeȝ disciplyne lest any tyme be wrattied þe lord: z ȝe pische fro þe rytuous wee. Whan hys wrath schal brennen out i schort. Blisful alle þat trosten in hym. Psalm þ whanne he schulde.

Lord whereto ben sterru fro þe fac of i multiplied þ tuo absolon hys sone slen me. manye inwardly rissen aȝeu me. Manye seyn to my soul: þ ys not heel to hy i hys god. Þou forsoy lord art myn vndertakere: my glorie z en hauncyge myn heued. Wt my vois to þe lord i ȝede: z he fulout herde me fro hys holy hil. I sleepte z was a slep z fulout

ros for þe lord vndertwc me. I schal not drede thousendis of puple goyge abunte me: ris vp lord mak me saf my god. For þ hast smyten alle doyge aduersite to me wtoute cause: þe teey of þe hsful þ hast tobrosid. Of þe lord ys helpe: z won þi puple þi blessyg. In þe i myȝaldy to þe wote þe psalm helpser ful out of þe sous of dauyd.

Whane me god of my rytuisnesse i tribulaciou þ spraddist out to me. Haue mcy of me z ful out here myn ori sou. Sones of me hou louste ȝe: sich wiȝt herte. wherto loue ȝee vanyte z seeken lesyg. And witee for þe lord hy wndi meruelous hys servet: þe lord ful out schal here me whanne I schal ben to hy. Wrathe ȝee z wiley not hy: þat ȝee seyn i ȝoure sertȝ z i ȝoure coucbis haue ȝe compuciou. Sacrifiȝey sacrifise of rytuisnesse z hopey i þe lord: manye seyn who schewe to vs gode thingis. Merked is vp on vs þe lyȝt of þi chere lord þ ȝeue gladnesse i myn herte. Of þe frute of whete wyn z oile of bȝ: þei ben multiplied. In pes i to itself: I schal slepe z resten. For þ lord synguler ly i hope hast togidere set me i to þi ende.

My wordis wt eris far for hir þat coyue þe lord vnder stonde myn cry. Ac heere to þe vois of myn orisou: my kig z my god. For to þee I schal preyn lord: erly þu ful out schalt here my vois. Erly I schal neeȝ stonde to þee z seen: for þu art god not willyst wickednesse. De schal dwelle beside ȝee þe schrewe: ne schul dwellen stille þe vnrytuise befor þyn eȝen. Þou hast hatid alle þat werke wickednesse: þu schalt leesen alle þat speke lesyg. Þe man of blodis z trecherous þe lord schal wlate. I forsoy i þe multitude of þi mcy. I schal entren i to þyn hous: I schal honou ȝe at þyn holy temple i þi drede. Lord bris fory me i þi rytuisnesse for myn enemys: mac redi i þi siȝte my wee. For þ ys not i þe mouy of he tieyr: þe herte of þe is veyn. An open sepulcre is þe þrote of þe: wt þeir tugis trecherouslý þei diden. deme ȝe þ þu god. Falle þei out fro þe thoȝtis: aftr þe multitude of þe vnpitousnessis of he put þem awey.

Trevisa, writing after Edward's death, attributes the change-over in part to the Black Death, which killed many French teachers who could not be replaced:

> ... so that now, the year of Our Lord 1385 ... in all the grammar-schools of England children leaveth the French and construeth and learneth English and have advantage on one side and disadvantage on the other. Their advantage is that they learn grammar in less time than children were wont to do; disadvantage is that now children of grammar-school know no more French than their left heel, and that is harm for them if they should pass the sea and travel in strange lands.

Some efforts, particularly at the universities, were made to keep up the study of French, and by the turn of the century we get the first French language textbooks. But the public drift was entirely the other way. In the 1350s the mayor and aldermen of London ordered that proceedings in the sheriff's courts there should be conducted in English; six years later the Chancellor opened Parliament for the first time in English, and it then enacted the Statute of Pleading. Henceforth, it said, 'as French is much unknown in the said realm ... the King ... hath ordained ... that all pleas which shall be pleaded in his courts whatsoever ... or in the courts and places of other lords whatsoever in the realm, shall be pleaded, showed, defended, answered, debated and judged in the English tongue ...'.

The English which thus replaced French was still in process of fashioning itself into a national language. Trevisa noted the difficulties posed by provincial dialects: 'the countray language is apayred, and som useth straunge wlafferynge, chiterynge, harrygne, and garrynge grisbayting'. North and south, he says, could not understand each other: only Midland folk could understand both. It was the East Midlands dialect, radiating from London, which thus became standard, the administrative change-over giving it enormous impetus.

The triumph of spoken English inevitably produced a vernacular literature. Of course, written English had never died out; but it reflected its rustic origins and its dependence on imported forms and themes. The Plantagenet state had hitherto recorded its achievements in Latin prose and French verse. But Edward's early victories produced the first Court propagandist writing in English, Laurence Minot, a northern poet whose vaunting patriotism reflected the mood of the times and was widely imitated. These are the verses Chaucer read in his youth. After the watershed of the 1350s, a new generation began to emerge, accustomed to regard their native tongue as a respectable vehicle for literary expression, and freed from the cultural tyranny of French, though not its influence. As in Elizabethan times, when the removal of the Latin yoke, in turn, opened new theatres for written English, the flowering of native talent was astonishingly swift and formidable. And it came from all over the country. Trevisa, the first man, almost, since Alfred to translate history into English, came from the west; Wyklif was the product of the Oxford culture; the unknown author of *Sir Gawayne and the Grene Knight* was a Lancashire man; Langland, whose first version of *Piers Plowman* dates from 1362, wrote in the West Midlands dialect. And Chaucer himself, whose genius was maturing as Edward sank into oblivion, was a man of London and the Court. He first appears, aged about twelve, in 1357, as a page to Edward's daughter-in-law, the Countess of Ulster; later he married one of Philippa's maids-of-honour, and soon emerged as an important official, courier, equerry, tax-official and diplomat, travelling widely on the King's business, captured in his service and ransomed by the King himself. Chaucer achieved his reputation in a Court whose daily language was now English, and whose evening delight was in the sophisticated poetry – French and Italian in inspiration, but emphatically English in expression – he had learned to produce. But in his last work, the unfinished *Canterbury Tales*, written when Edward himself was only a memory, he embraces an entire cross-section of the nation which the King had brought into consciousness: knight and squire, miller and yeoman, ploughman and poor scholar, housewife and prioress, monk and priest, merchant and shipman, weaver, carpenter, cook and publican. From the great wars, the English were emerging as a nation, but a nation of individuals nonetheless, their separate images indelibly described by a great national poet, in a language all could understand.

7 The Attrition of War 1351-77

IF THE WAR BROUGHT indirect and inestimable benefits to the English people, by force-feeding their national self-respect and liberating their language and culture, any direct material gains are much harder to discern. Final victory, or a durable peace, proved equally elusive. After his triumphs at Crécy, Calais and Winchelsea, Edward might reasonably have expected a peace which would have maintained the *status quo* in Gascony – his only real, long-term aim – for many years. But a number of factors made a resumption of the war almost inevitable. The 'political nation' in England had, for the moment, good reason to believe the conflict profitable. The more active aristocrats had undoubtedly made fortunes during the 1340s, and war as a career offered opportunities to many lesser men, some of very humble origin. Edward's own eldest son was now fully of age, and invested with growing responsibilities. He seems always to have been in debt, no doubt because he preferred warfare and Court display, where he shone, to estate-administration, for which he had no talent. He, at least, had strong financial motives for resuming the fighting. Then, too, the English government had reason to think that the internal state of France favoured more annexations. Edward had a new ally, the King of Navarre, known to the French as Charles the Bad. Bad or good, he was certainly unreliable, as Edward found to his cost: but he offered tempting proposals for a final division of France between himself and the English King. The moment might be ripe. The Black Death had struck France no more heavily than England, but its economic and social consequences were more serious. Whereas, in England, the new freedom of the labourer, and his rise in real wages, had been feebly resisted by Parliament, and in effect accepted by the landed class, in France brutal, even desperate, efforts were made to reimpose the feudal mould, and these in turn provoked peasant rebellions and *jacqueries*. At times in the 1350s, large parts of France were ungovernable, and ungoverned.

Yet the new French King, John, who succeeded in 1350, was an optimist and, in his own foolish way, ambitious. There were, in fact, strong political reasons for him to wish to reverse the defeats of the 1340s, just as there were strong military and economic reasons which made this impossible. He was impressed by the collapse of Edward's position in Flanders, where the new

172

King John at the battle of Poitiers where he
was heavily defeated and captured. He was
taken to England, to a comfortable
imprisonment in Windsor Castle, while his
ransom was arranged.

count, Louis de Male, his ally, resolved his differences with the towns, and got recognition from them. John rejected the advice and efforts of Innocent IV to make a final peace, and allowed the truce to lapse. Hostilities, which had never really died down, broke out at a number of points.

In 1355 Edward resumed large-scale action by taking an expedition to Calais, but he was home in November after two months. Meanwhile in September, the Black Prince, who was now his lieutenant in Gascony, ravaged the south and the Mediterranean provinces, hitherto untouched by the war, returning to base with rich plunder. In 1356 he decided to resume the operation in central and north-west France, repeating his Father's strategy of inflicting unacceptable damage on France's economy, with the object of bringing the French King to battle. The pattern of Crécy re-emerged, with emphatic variations. He left Bordeaux on 6 July, with two thousand men-at-arms and a force of archers variously computed at between four and six thousand, including a mounted division of three hundred. There were also fifteen hundred of what the French termed 'brigands', presumably the hated Welsh footmen. The Prince crossed the Dordogne and the Loire, taking and plundering open towns and avoiding strongly fortified centres; he got as far as Bourges, which was too much for him, so he burned its suburbs, as usual, and began to retreat to Bordeaux. It was at this point, early in September, that he became aware that the French King, with a very large force – possibly as many as fifty thousand men – was to the south of him, across his line of retreat.

Intelligence on both sides seems to have been faulty, and the armies eventually blundered into contact with each other near Poitiers, on Saturday 17 September. The Prince then evidently decided either that John would not now be able to resist the temptation to attack, or that a fight was inevitable. He chose a very strong defensive position, on high ground, with access only through a narrow lane bordered by hedges. French scouts later reported that the lane could take only four men-at-arms abreast. The Prince put his archers in the hedges and his men-at-arms at the top, but he kept mounted in reserve both a division of armoured troops and his horse-archers.

John was well-informed of the strength of the English

position, and under pressure from a papal mission to negotiate a truce. Talks between both sides, with a cardinal as intermediary, in fact took place throughout Sunday, but terms could not be agreed, and in the meantime the English dug ditches and turned their position into a fortified camp. John showed some recognition of English tactics by ordering his men-at-arms to attack dismounted, but he does not seem to have controlled the battle, which began, as usual, by accident. The first French division became involved, piecemeal, in the lane, was broken by the archers and retreated, colliding with the divisions behind it. The Black Prince then varied his father's tactics by moving out of the camp with cavalry, to savage the confused armoured footmen. King John's position was still essentially strong, in that his own huge division was intact. But he lacked the flexibility which wins battles: continuing the tactic of fighting on foot, which made some sense against archers, he made the preposterous mistake of advancing dismounted, in the open, against the English cavalry. French casualties were enormous. John himself lost his liberty, together with thirteen counts, an archbishop, sixty-six barons and bannerets, and two thousand men-at-arms. John was taken with the army to Bordeaux, and in April 1357, after a two-year truce was arranged, brought under heavy escort to London, and then to Windsor, while the terms of his ransom were arranged.

From this astonishing stroke of fortune, the English did their best to extract a workable peace. Edward seems all along to have been willing to renounce his royal claim, provided the territorial terms were acceptable. France, governed by the discredited Duke of Normandy, who had fled from Poitiers, with a nineteen-year-old Dauphin on the throne, a *jacquerie* in virtual possession of Paris, and armed bands of peasants and 'free' captains roaming the countryside, put up a surprisingly stiff legal resistance. In 1359–60, Edward himself, to deliver the *coup de grace*, took a ravaging expedition through the heart of France, and forced the Duke of Burgundy to buy neutrality. He had some bad luck, failing to take Rheims, but he succeeded in his object of bringing the French to terms. By a treaty negotiated at Brétigny, near Chartres, in May 1360, subsequently endorsed by both Kings at Calais in October, he got most of what he wanted. He was awarded full sovereignty over

Gascony, the disputed border territories, Poitou, Calais and its march, and other lands in northern France. John was to be released after payment of a first instalment of 600,000 gold crowns (£100,000), the full ransom being set at 3,000,000. In return, Edward renounced his claim to the French throne.

The Treaty of Brétigny-Calais proved abortive, both for reasons which reflect discredit on the two parties, and for others beyond their control. When it was signed, the mutual re-nunciation of sovereignty provisions were put in a separate document, with a new proviso that the treaty should be carried out not later than 1 November 1361. This suggests that both sides were dissatisfied with the terms, and anxious to keep open

Pillagers carrying away bows from Vitry.

OVERLEAF The battle of Poitiers.

177

tum nostrum

Recordatus est quoniam puluis
sumus: homo sicut fenum dies eius
tanquam flos agri sic efflorebit.

Quoniam spiritus pertransibit in
illo + non subsistet: + non cognoscet
amplius locum suum

Misericordia autem domini ab eter
no: + usque in eternum super timen
tes eum

Et iusticia illius in filios filiorū:
hiis qui seruant testamentum eius.

Et memores sunt mandatorum
ipsius: ipsius: ad faciendum ea.

a: et erultauimus et delectati sumus in

.Constantinus.   .Nobilis.

Scenes from the *Luttrell Psalter*, *c.* 1340.
LEFT The royal coach; the lady looking out
may represent Queen Philippa.
ABOVE Town life in East Anglia.
TOP A dining scene.
BELOW Townsfolk doing the round dance

a loophole for resuming the fight, especially since the short period allowed for implementing the basic treaty raised severe practical difficulties. The transfer of the disputed territories was an immensely complicated business, involving a variety of acute local issues, factions and personalities, not least the free captains on both sides, who were virtually independent and who held many of the castles, towns and villages involved. In fact it could not be done, certainly in the allotted time, and it was not done. Thus at any time from the end of 1361 both sides had ample pretext to declare the treaty unfulfilled and resume the fighting. Between the two Kings themselves there was a certain amount of goodwill. John was handsomely treated as a prisoner, at Windsor and elsewhere, and for most of the time he was allowed to hunt in the vast Windsor forest, then stretching for over two hundred square miles. Edward allowed him to go home after only 400,000 crowns of the ransom had been paid, leaving his three sons as hostages; when one of these, the Duke of Anjou, broke his parole, John felt that he had to return, and died still a prisoner in April 1364. But for the younger generation – the Black Prince, and John's Dauphin and successor Charles V – a return to war seemed to offer many advantages and opportunities. Unlike his father, the Prince, in Bordeaux, was faced with the practical difficulties of maintaining the territorial integrity, and the revenues, of the duchy of Aquitaine, as settled by the treaty. Charles had the challenge of restoring the kingdom which was scarcely half the size of the one his father had inherited. In many parts of France, fighting continued from time to time: war had become a business for the free captains and their men, and the money they had become accustomed to receiving from royal indentures was now replaced by the profits of private military enterprise.

There was also the widespread belief, shared to some extent by Parliament, and passionately held by the military aristocracy and gentry, that war was a profitable business. The English suffered little directly from the conflict. Casualties were few and, compared with the ravages of the plague, insignificant. There were a few raids on coastal towns, but no French army ever established itself on the mainland; Scotland was still a threat, but a distant one; Edward always received the thanks of Parliament for his success in maintaining 'the peace of the realm'. It is true there was a high level of internal disorder, and that this tended to increase, as unemployed knights and soldiers returned from the war, and took an active interest in internal disputes. There were many complaints on this score. But then there always had been complaints. The English ruling class lived uneasily on the borderline of legality. Thus, an examination of the personalities and records of the Bedfordshire Members of Parliament during the decade 1327–37, before the war had begun, shows that seven out of twelve had at one time or another been accused of serious offences, ranging from theft and housebreaking to the murder of a coroner. What the wars did was to help to spread the habits of lawlessness among the poorer classes, and we read occasionally of entire villages, organised no doubt by ex-soldiers, resisting royal or baronial officials.

Against this were set the direct profits of the war, which were visible and much talked about. A great deal of portable booty, robbed from churches, abbeys, manors and towns, made its way from France to England. Prisoners were stripped of their personal possessions, often of considerable value. The Chandos Herald praises the Black Prince for the extraordinary courtesy with which he treated King John when he was captured, insisting on serving his meals personally, on his knees. But the Prince nonetheless robbed his prisoner of his jewels. More rewarding, however, was the ransom racket, the trade in human livestock. It had the merit of sparing lives, at any rate of the better-off (non-ransomable prisoners were given short shrift); but the huge ransoms demanded, and often obtained, had ultimately to be extracted from the peasants, thus adding to the burden war imposed on the poorer classes. Elaborate rules governed the question of ransoms. Civilians captured in the storming of cities were as liable as combatants. A burgess could be ransomed for axes, swords, coats, doublets and horses – the last in some ways the most valuable form of booty, always easy to dispose of in a seller's market. Knights paid in horses and money. As the social scale rose, so did the ransom. Wealthy men speculated in prisoners, who could be bought and sold; Calais became a sort of emporium for this trade. In 1347 Sir Thomas Dagworth was offered £4,900 for Charles of Blois, the French-supported Breton pretender. Sir

Bodiam Castle, Sussex, built by Sir Edward Dalyngrigge with his fortune made in the French wars.

John Harleston sold his share of one French knight, taken in Normandy, for £1,583.6.8. Edward, in particular, engaged heavily in the trade, for it paid him to buy up valuable prisoners cheap for cash, since he had means to enforce collection of ransoms. Thus, he bought up a job lot of the Black Prince's Poitiers prisoners for £20,000. He paid Sir John Wingfield £1,666.13.4 for the Sire Daubigny, Sir Thomas Cheyne £1,483.6.8 for Bertrand Duguesclin, captured at Nájera, and Sir Thomas Holland 20,000 marks for the Count of Eu. Sometimes the deals had the complexity beloved of medieval man: Edward gave Robert Clinton £700 plus a parcel of Irish manors (probably of little value), for a fourth share of the ransom of the Archbishop of Le Mans. If prelates were ransomable, this is not surprising: they were present at all the major engagements, and often gave the most bloodthirsty advice on the eve of battle.

In theory, a soldier paid one-third of his profits for ransoms to his captain, who in turn paid the Crown a third of such profits, plus a third of his own. Edward reserved to himself royal prisoners and commanders-in-chief: but the man who actually made such captures was handsomely rewarded. Thus John Coupland, who took David II at Neville's Cross, got an annuity of £500 and the rank of banneret. There were black market deals. An archer named John Ballard captured the Archdeacon of Paris, deserted, smuggled his prisoner to London and sold him for £50; this case came to light, but many others did not. A black market prisoner was at risk, for he might be killed and buried to avoid detection. There were also disputes over who exactly made the capture. Two knights claimed to have captured King John at Poitiers; the Black Prince, says Froissart, ended the argument by saying: 'I am so great a lord as to make you both rich.'

Many, indeed, did become rich. The Earl of Arundel, old 'Copped Hat', who fought at Sluys, Winchelsea and Crécy, left £60,000 in cash and bullion when he died. A variety of evidence shows that the fighting aristocrats raised their living-standards through the war, and this is reflected in the sumptuous castles, such as Bodiam, which they were allowed to build – Edward was generous in this respect, issuing over 180 licences to crenellate. The captains did even better. Robert Salle was a

A prosperous yeoman and his lady.

bondman in 1335, when he was conscripted; thirty years later he was a knight and commander of a Calais fort; his will, made in 1380, reveals him as a rich man (one of the reasons why he was murdered by the peasants the next year). Such astonishing success-stories, a bitter, puritanical consciousness that money was falling into the wrong hands – not merely through battle, but by mercantile war-profits – prompted the sumptuary laws,

185

which laid down in impossible detail what people were to wear and eat. Under the statute of 1363, grooms and servants of lords were to get meat or fish only once a day – otherwise scraps. They were to wear cloth costing not more than 13s 4d for a whole suit, their wives and children the same; silk and gold, silver and enamel embroidery were forbidden. Yeomen and tradesmen could wear clothes up to £2 in value, but were likewise forbidden silk and embroidery, and any buttons, decorative daggers, rings, jewels, collars or chains made of gold and silver. Their wives' veils had to be made of yarn, not silk, and they were forbidden lambskin or furs, except rabbit, cat or fox. Carters, ploughmen and herds were forbidden even cloth, being restricted to blanket or homespun wool, costing 12d or less; they were to 'eat and drink in the same manner that pertains to them, and not excessively' – an indication that, at this point, the Parliamentary draftsman gave up. The well-to-do were also restricted, and in a manner characteristic of English landed snobbery: thus merchants with £1,000 were treated as equivalent to squires and gentlemen of £200. Such legislation indicates that, whether or not the wars actually increased the total wealth of England, they led to its widespread redistribution.

The effect of the war on the English economy is hard to calculate, because it cannot be isolated from other factors, notably the consequences of plague. In its earlier decades, it undoubtedly gave a crucial stimulus to the English cloth trade, which had hitherto been confined to a few speciality lines. The number of English cloths produced more than quadrupled during the reign, and the industry survived the depression years of the 1370s, when the inruption of the French army into Gascony destroyed the purchasing power of England's best export market, Bordeaux and its hinterland. One undoubted casualty of the war was the Bordeaux wine trade. In Edward's early days, claret was remarkably cheap in England, and the King himself was supplied on even easier terms. England took twenty-five per cent of the hundred thousand tuns annually exported from Bordeaux, and two thousand tuns went to the King, in the form of a *prise*, for which he paid only 20s freight per tun. The war destroyed many of the vineyards, and after 1369 the trade came practically to a standstill. Even when the wine could be produced, naval warfare and the piracy it

encouraged forced the wine-ships to travel in convoy, and so raised the freight price. Though there was some recovery in the 1380s, claret never went back to its pre-war cheapness: the net effect of the conflict was to double its price, from £3 to £6 a tun.

But of course the chief sufferers were French peasants, and those who lived in ill-defended towns. The wars were not continuous, otherwise France could not have survived at all. From 1337–77, active war engaged only a third of the time, truce and unratified peace the rest. But truces could not always be enforced, even at the personal intervention of the King. Moreover, when active war was resumed, the destruction of the French economy – and thus the tax revenue of the French

The seal die of the wool staple in Westminster.

187

Crown – became the prime object of English strategy. The chroniclers repeatedly describe the way in which the English forces looted and then burned captured towns. Less often noted, but more important economically, was the destruction of the villages. The armies appropriated all stored food found in their line of march, burned what they could not carry, and then set fire to barns, boats, mills, stables, carts and houses – virtually all of wood. This was the pattern from the start. When Edward planned to invade northern France in the autumn of 1339, the French-born Cardinal de Montfavez of the papal mission tried to dissuade him on the grounds that 'The Kingdom of France is surrounded by a silken thread, which all the power of England is not enough to break.' Edward promptly invaded with twelve thousand men, and a few days later Sir Geoffrey Scrope, one of the King's judges, took the Cardinal to the top of a high tower, and showed him 'the whole countryside of France, for a distance of 15 miles, burning everywhere, and said: "Sir, does it not seem to you that the silken thread surrounding France is broken?"' As the wars continued, atrocities

became more frequent. In theory, the laws of war protected clergy and peasants. Early in his campaigns, Edward once had twenty soldiers hanged for robbing a church. But in 1373 an eyewitness said that he had seen Sir John Harleston, one of the King's leading generals, feasting his men from over a hundred stolen chalices of church plate. The heraldic writer Honoré Bonet notes in his *Tree of Battles*: 'In these days all wars are directed against poor labouring people.' French armies behaved no better than the English, and the free bands worse than either. There were mass rapes, and peasants and farmers were hanged and roasted alive to disgorge hidden stores of grain or gold. In his treatise on war, *De Re Militari*, Paris de Pozo admits: 'A man may not torture a prisoner to extort money from him by way of ransom, but with peasants it is different, at least according to the custom of the mercenaries.'

Though bishops blessed and accompanied the armies on both sides, some clergymen spoke out hotly against the war. Philippe de Mezières, referring to the English free companies, claimed that the English were a scourge inflicted by God on the French

Peasants hoeing, from the *Luttrell Psalter*. They were the chief sufferers in the Hundred Years' War because of the continual ravaging of the land by marauding forces.

The battle of Poitiers.

190

sommes mors lay encores mon
mon pire et de beaulx freres et
auffi vous aues de bons amis qui
nous contreuengeront. Si vous
prie que vous vueilles humente

The coronation of
Charles v of France.

for punishment for their own sins. In 1375, Thomas Brinton of Rochester, a radical critic of the war, said that recent English reverses were a divine visitation for their past offences in ruining France. There was a distinct minority opinion in England, represented by such diverse figures as John Bromyard, the orthodox Dominican, Wyklif, the heresiarch, and Walter Brut, a prominent layman and landowner, who opposed the war as such, and said so.

As time passed, the attrition of war itself defeated English strategy. After the defeat at Poitiers, the French state began to reorganise itself on a defensive basis, a process accelerated by the shrewd and methodical Charles V. New forms of taxation were devised, collected by a new class of officials directly answerable to the Crown. A standing army was created, seigneurial castles were occupied and strengthened by the royal forces, and semi-independent baronial honours integrated into the state. Under Charles V, we see the first, faint adumbrations of the French absolute monarchy. Whereas in England, the war force-fed the development of constitutional and Parliamentary forms, in France there was a reverse process, the *Parlement* gradually ceasing to be, as in England, a conclave of amateur politicians, and becoming a court of professional lawyers. But in one vital respect, the war had a similar impact: the maturing of nationalism. If England was becoming a nation, so, more slowly, was France, and a much bigger and more powerful one. The key English strategy, the devastation of the French countryside, gradually brought about an internal immigration of French peasants into the fortified towns, especially those defended and guaranteed by the French Crown; and the new and enlarged towns were engines of French nationalism, and of a new, direct relationship between subject and monarch. This process applied not merely to those territories which had always owed allegiance to the French royal House, but increasingly, granted a common language and culture, to the French lands of the English King. These forces became ominously manifest in the last decade of Edward's reign: and they coincided with a collapse of authority at the very heart of the English state – in the King's own person.

OPPOSITE The tree of Jesse, from the Ormesby Psalter. (MS Douce 366 f 9v.)

8
Twilight and Darkness
1364-77

SOMETIME BEFORE DECEMBER 1364, Alice Perrers became Edward's mistress. He had had love affairs before, but they were short-lived and attracted little comment, and certainly no scandal. What made his liaison with Alice different was its durability, and her strong character. By October 1366 she was officially installed as a maid of the Queen's bedchamber, implying that Philippa had given, willingly or not, her sanction to a permanent arrangement. About the same time the records show that the King granted her two tuns of wine, and thereafter she received wardships (which had a straight cash value), lands and jewels, plus, in 1371, the valuable manor of Wendover. Very little is known about this woman, and most of our information comes from the virulently hostile source of the St Albans Chronicle. According to this, she was the daughter of an Essex tiler and a former domestic servant, and made her way to Court by very humble channels. The chronicler adds that she was extremely ugly, and ruled the King through her clever tongue. (This last is possible: Edward liked his women to be clever, as well as attractive.) The truth seems to be that she was the daughter of a prominent Hertfordshire landowner, Sir Richard Perrers, who was frequently MP and sheriff for the county; her arrival at Court would thus be perfectly natural, for the King had strong Hertfordshire connections. Unfortunately, Sir Richard fell foul of St Albans Abbey – a common fate of those whose lands marched with the estates of a powerful monastery – and as a result of the dispute was imprisoned and outlawed for a time. This litigation, to which by 1374 Alice herself was an active party, envenomed the chronicler's account; and certainly explains why he accused her of the monstrous offence of taking her place on the judicial bench and trying to bully the judges.

There is also a dispute about her marriage. One account states that she was married twice. She certainly went through a form of marriage to Sir William de Windsor, one of the castle officials. On 2 June 1374 the huge sum of £1,615.3.11 was paid through her into his hands; and Edward twice sent him as lieutenant to Ireland, a place in which he took little interest, no doubt to get Windsor off the scene. The canon law of marriage was so complex that it was often difficult for people to know whether or not they had contracted a valid marriage, which

PREVIOUS PAGES, LEFT
The funeral effigy of
Edward III, presumably
taken from his death mask
as it shows one side of his
mouth twisted with
paralysis. RIGHT The
serene head of the King
from his monument in
Westminster Abbey.

could be overthrown by a decision in the clerical courts decades after it had taken place. Edward believed her to be unmarried: when the Commons petitioned against her in 1376, and told the King she was married to Windsor, he 'swore with an oath' that he knew nothing of it. Alice certainly became a wealthy woman, and continued to litigate vigorously until her death at the end of 1400. She had two daughters, Jane and Joan, to whom she left a good deal of money; she had financial dealings with such grandees as John of Gaunt, William of Wykeham and Lord Latimer; and she owned Egremont Castle and valuable property in London. What we know suggests that she was a woman of conspicuous ability, who fought hard for herself and her sex in a man's world – and that Edward respected her for it.

None of this would have mattered, if Edward had remained an active monarch. But Edward slipped into a long dotage, made more difficult for the authorities to deal with because it was so gradual in its impact, and because the King could, if forced, rouse himself from his lethargy almost till the end. There was thus no question of a regency, or of any other formal arrangement to fill the growing vacuum at the centre of government. Edward was never his own self after the desperate winter campaign of 1359–60, marked by appalling weather, in which men and horses died of cold and starvation. From 1362 he became much less active. He kept up his hunting, but he neglected administrative work. Probably he was drinking too much; but it may be, also, that with failing health and suffering intensely from the cold, he found the formal life of his major palaces irksome. He spent less and less time at Windsor (notoriously drafty) and Westminster, where privacy was impossible, and more at his comfortable domestic palaces and hunting-boxes, such as Eltham, Richmond and Havering. Almost his last visit to Windsor was in August 1369, to be present at Philippa's deathbed. Her removal was a heavy blow to him. Despite his infidelities, they had remained on excellent terms, and he depended greatly on her for advice and encouragement. When he reached her bedside, she took him by the hand, and made certain small requests about her will and debts, which he granted, in tears. Then, says Froissart:

> The good lady and Queen made on her the sign of the cross, and commended the King her husband to God, and her youngest son

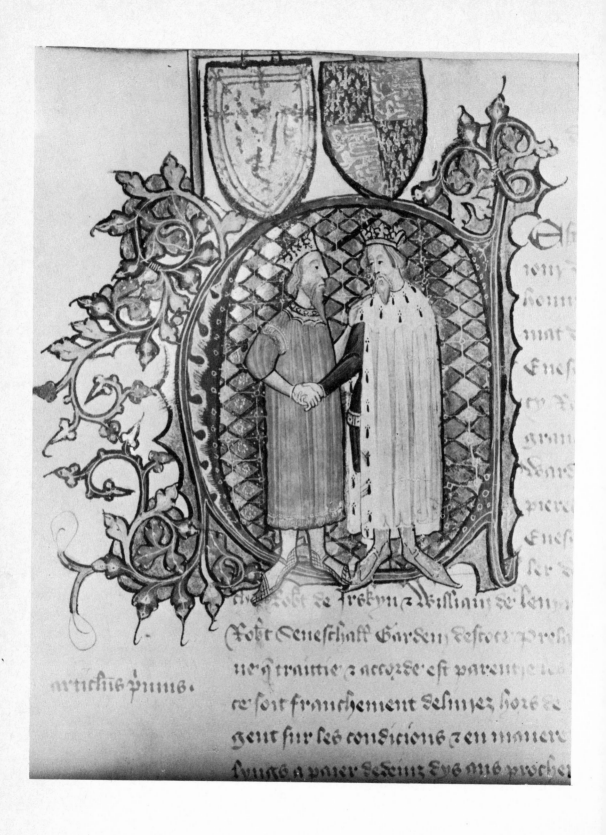

Thomas, who was there beside her. And anon, after, she yielded up the spirit, the which I believe surely the holy angels received with great joy up to heaven, for in all her life she did neither in thought nor deed anything whereby to lose her soul, as far as any creature could know.

With the removal of Philippa, and her strong sense of the responsibilities of kingship, Edward's decline accelerated. He was later accused of giving Alice Philippa's jewels; this seems unlikely, though his presents to his mistress, as always with Edward, were munificent. What does emerge from the records is that his visits to London became rare, and were carried out in secret, usually to transact private business. Edward was now an old man by medieval standards; but age had not prevented his grandfather from retaining his iron grip on administrative routine, and there is a temptation to draw sinister parallels with the lassitude of his father. As late as the autumn of 1372, he made a final effort to go on campaign again, boarding his ship the *Grace Dieu* at Sandwich; but after six weeks, continuing bad weather forced him to disembark. Thereafter, he could barely stir himself even to open Parliaments.

The inactivity of the King coincided with, and reinforced, a progressive deterioration in England's international position. Edward's military efforts had always been underpinned by vigorous diplomacy throughout western Europe. After 1360, the dynamic began to run down. Scotland drifted back into the French camp. The capture of David II had not ended Scottish hostility, the nationalists continuing to fight under the leadership of Robert the Steward, founder of the Stuart line. When Edward sent David home with a ten-year truce, in return for a ransom of 100,000 crowns, he failed to persuade the Scots to accept an English paramountcy. David had no children, and disliked Steward, his heir-presumptive. But his proposal, in 1364, for a union of the Scottish and English crowns was rejected by the Scots Parliament; and when Steward succeeded him in 1371, almost his first act was to conclude a formal alliance with Charles V, the beginning of a diplomatic nexus which was to cause English governments continual anxiety until the late sixteenth century.

In Ireland, the nominal rule of the English Crown contracted. Lionel, Duke of Clarence, Edward's son and Irish lieutenant,

OPPOSITE King Edward with King David of Scotland, who was eventually freed for a ransom of 100,000 crowns. His pro-English policy was rejected by the Scots parliament and reversed by his successor, who in 1371 made an alliance with France.

died in 1368; but even before his death, the Statutes of Kilkenny confessed the defeat of English policy, since they implicitly conceeded that the King's writ ran only in a restricted area around Dublin, and concentrated on protecting English settlers from Irish 'degeneracy', by what amounted to a system of apartheid. When Edward sent William de Windsor there as lieutenant in 1369, the appointment of such an insignificant official provoked an outcry, and he had to be recalled two years later. In 1374, for personal reasons, the King sent him back to Dublin, where he engaged in acrimonious and futile efforts to persuade the Anglo-Irish to pay their taxes. In Edward's reign, as always, Ireland was the graveyard of English statesmanship.

There were further reverses along the periphery of the French state. Edward had hoped to resurrect the Anglo-Flemish coalition by marrying his fifth son, Edmund of Langley, Duke of Cambridge, to Margaret, the only child of Louis de Male, and heiress to Flanders, Artois and imperial Burgundy. But this scheme, like so many medieval marriages, required a dispensation, and Charles v persuaded the pro-French Pope, Urban v, to refuse it; worse, in 1369 he succeeded in marrying Margaret to his own brother, Philip, Duke of French Burgundy, which – for the present at least – sealed off any threat to the French Crown from the north and east. Even in Brittany, where the pro-French claimant, Charles of Blois, was killed in 1364, the French gained ground; for the new Duke, John de Montfort, though nominally the English candidate, found in practice that it was more convenient to do homage to Charles v, and English mercenaries had to be withdrawn.

This left Charles free to concentrate on Gascony. As Duke, the Black Prince had enjoyed a good deal of local popularity in the early 1360s. Of his Court, the Chandos Herald wrote: 'there abode all nobleness, all joy and jollity, largesse, gentleness and honour, and all his subjects and all his men loved him right dearly'. But Gascony, like many other parts of France, had suffered heavily in the war, and the Prince's efforts to collect taxes, especially the hated *fouage*, or hearth-tax, aroused resistance; he was criticised, too, for giving the best jobs to his English friends, rather than Gascons – thus antagonising the growing French nationalism of the duchy. In 1366 the Prince was obliged to shoulder fresh responsibilities in Spain, where a

OPPOSITE A banquet given by Charles v for the Emperor Charles iv.

mement eft la renesch
de Reims Cupies seoit
lempirisis Capies seoit
le Roy andresne on nuheu
du front de la sale Capies
le Roy de frñce seoir le roy

des romains. Et auoit autãt de distance
du Roy au Roy des romains cõe du
Roy a lempirir. Et anoient lempreu
le Roy et le Roy des romains chascun se
parement vn ciel de drap dor borde de velu
au aus armes de frãce. et par dessus ceul

disputed succession to Castile posed a pro-French claimant, the bastard Henry of Trastamara, against the legitimate King Peter, whose co-heiresses were married into the English royal family. The French called him Peter the Cruel; cruel or kind, he certainly proved an English liability. The Black Prince's Spanish intervention was presented by his apologists as motivated by chivalry and morality. In fact it was a hard-headed calculation, whose principal object was to deny France the support of the Castilian navy. In February 1367 the Black Prince moved his army into Spain, crossing the Pyrenees passes in appalling weather. It was, in a way, his most courageous campaign, for he was desperately short of cash. Always improvident, his custom had been to buy jewelry in his moments of affluence – he once paid £1,883.6.8 for a single ruby – for sale at times of crisis. Now he pooled his liquid resources with those of Peter, but their attempts to dispose of so much jewelry quickly flooded the market, and their assets had to be sold at knock-down prices. Even so, on 3 April, the Prince won a remarkable victory over the Castilians at Nájera, and installed Peter in triumph.

But this was his high-water mark. Soon after the battle, the Prince contracted dropsy, and returned to Bordeaux. Peter proved incapable of reuniting the Castilian nobility, and two years later contrived to get himself killed. Thereafter, the handling of English affairs in Spain devolved upon John of Gaunt, who had married one of Peter's coheiresses; he was a skilled financier and diplomat, but no soldier. The Black Prince was now saddled with a mountain of debt, and from the beginning of 1369 became so ill that he was unable to ride. To settle his debts, he ordered a new Gascon *fouage*, and this provoked two of his nobles, the lords of Armagnac and Albret, to appeal over his head to the French Court – the classic detonator of war. On 3 December 1368, Charles V accepted the appeal, thus breaking the Treaty of Paris. The English government responded with the only legal sanction it possessed, and next summer Edward resumed the title of King of France. In November, Charles confiscated his French territories.

Quite apart from the deficiencies in English leadership, objective factors were heavily in Charles's favour. Except in Bordeaux itself, the Gascons now leaned towards the French Crown. Among many other reverses, Limoges was treacherously surrendered to the French by its bishop, whom the Black Prince had trusted. In a terrible outburst of anger, he swore 'by the soul of his father', that he would revenge himself on its inhabitants. He besieged the city, directing operations from a litter, and in considerable pain. It took the whole of October 1370 to mine the walls, and when a breach was made, the Prince ordered no quarter. Over three thousand citizens were butchered, though paradoxically the life of the bishop, on the advice of John of Gaunt, was spared. This was the Prince's last effort. In January 1371 he returned to England, and went into virtual retirement at his manor of Berkhamsted; he resigned his French position in October 1372, giving lack of money as his chief reason. As a soldier, politician and administrator he was finished, though his shadow hovered over the English scene until his death in 1376.

Edward's family was now much diminished, though its survivors remained on close terms. The chief responsibility devolved on John of Gaunt, who was much preoccupied with his Spanish affairs. After the Black Prince's retirement, the Gascon border territories were occupied by the French, and Brittany overrun, thus imperilling the English sea-lanes, in both Biscay and the Channel. Two great *chevauchées*, or cavalry ravages, were conducted through France by Sir Robert Knollys and John of Gaunt himself: they inflicted terrible damage, and seized a good deal of booty, but they did not change the strategic position. Indeed, the advantage passed to the French and their Castilian allies, notably at sea. Despite his naval victories, Edward had made no consistent effort to build up a regular navy, or the docks and services needed to maintain it. In 1337 he had created the structure of a naval command by appointing two admirals, one north and one west of the Thames; an admiralty court had emerged in mid-century, and a new coin, the golden noble, had been introduced in 1344, showing the King standing on a ship with his sword and shield. But these were gestures; the reality was that Edward continued to rely for his naval forces on impressed merchantmen and ships hired from Genoa and elsewhere in Italy. The number of the King's ships actually at sea never exceeded twenty-seven; and in the 1370s England was faced with a combined professional navy, including Spanish galleys which could move close

205

inshore. In 1372, off La Rochelle, the English fleet, commanded by the young Earl of Pembroke, was decisively beaten by the Castilians, and for the rest of Edward's reign the Franco-Spanish allies enjoyed relative superiority even in the Channel. By the time a two-year truce was negotiated in 1375, England's possessions in France had been reduced to Calais and the Bordeaux-Bayonne coastal strip; and when the truce lapsed in 1377, the French and Spanish immediately began raids on the English coast, burning Rye and Hastings. Indeed, England's military efforts in the 1370s were largely defensive, concentrating on the construction of a new generation of southern castles and walled ports.

Thus Edward's reign drew to its close amid military reverses, and these in turn provoked political crisis. Parliament had never been a docile instrument in Edward's hands: but so long as he was active, it was broadly under control, and in particular Edward had always been able to maintain a balance between the clerical and secular forces in the 'political nation'. By the early 1370s, however, he – the 'chief and first estate' of Parliament – was virtually an absentee. Of his sons, Lionel was dead, the Black Prince out of action, Edmund a nonentity, Thomas too young and John of Gaunt often abroad. The government was in the hands of Court bishops, Wykeham of Winchester, the Chancellor, and Brantingham of Exeter, the Treasurer. Wykeham was personally acceptable to the magnates, for even those who most criticised him did not attack his character. But he was not popular, and the King's increasing dependence on him – 'all things,' says Froissart, 'were done by him and without him nothing was done' – was widely resented. He had made his way to preferment by his building activities at Windsor: Wyklif sneered at him as 'a clerk wise in building castles'. Edward had fought a bitter battle with the Pope to create him Bishop of Winchester, and, as bishop, his very able administration of his estates had made him one of the wealthiest men in England. Clerical wealth, indeed, was an issue, for the Commons, faced with military defeat and the need to raise ever-larger sums in taxation – the Bordeaux revenues were now virtually written off – claimed vociferously that the clergy were being under-taxed. In fact, Edward in his own devious way had milked the clergy heavily; but it may be that, as his grip

just mention a brief outline, & don't copy it all out, 3/4 in bull-shitting.

OPPOSITE The effigy of the Black Prince from his tomb in Canterbury Cathedral.

weakened, and with clericalists controlling the two chief departments, pressure on the clergy had been relaxed. At all events, when Parliament met in 1371, the Lords dismissed Wykeham and Brantingham, Edward weakly assenting.

Their offices were filled by laymen and judges, Sir Robert Thorpe, Sir Richard Scrope and later Sir John Knyvet, men loosely attached to the Lancastrian interest, which once more asserted itself as the countervailing force to royal power. Indeed, in so far as the new government had a political complexion, it was coloured by John of Gaunt, and tinged with anti-clericalism. But it was no more successful than its predecessor, either in pursuing the war or in reducing taxation. In 1372 Parliament expressed its mistrust of the authorities by excluding lawyers and sheriffs, thus threatening the government's 'natural' support in the Commons. The next year, the knights and burgesses refused to vote a subsidy until they were granted a conference with the Lords, in which they criticised the royal Chamberlain, Lord Latimer, customs officials and the small group of merchants who farmed sections of the revenue. In 1374 and 1375 it was thought too risky to summon Parliament at all. The truce with France finally arranged in 1375 provoked an outcry. It involved the abandonment of two key fortresses for which Latimer was formally responsible, Becherel in Brittany and St Sauveur in Normandy; and it came into effect just as the English were about to take Quimperle in Brittany, thus robbing them of a morale-boosting victory. Moreover, the negotiations had been conducted by Gaunt in an expensive and ostentatious manner, which the Commons thought unseemly in the circumstances. Walsingham writes of '*horribiles expenses and incredibiles*', and the York Chronicler of '*graunt despens et graunt riot ... pur reveler et dauncer*', giving the cost as £20,000.

When Parliament finally had to be summoned in April 1376, a wholly new situation began to develop. Edward met them in the Painted Chamber at Westminster, but immediately withdrew. The Lords then reassembled in the White Chamber, and the Commons in the Chapter House of the Abbey, bringing with them a mountain of petitions, ranging over the whole activities of government, and couched in strong language. The *Anonimalle Chronicle* gives a detailed account of the Commons proceedings, which began with the imposition of an oath of mutual loyalty and secrecy, and the appointment of a Speaker, Sir Peter de la Mare. There was no apparent precedent for such actions, or, indeed, for the manner in which the Commons had taken the political lead. They refused adamantly to vote the subsidies requested – despite a message from the King for action – until their petitions were answered, and to reinforce this they asked for the formation of a joint committee of the Houses, to include anti-Court magnates and bishops, to work for administrative reform. In addition, they brought particular charges against Latimer, Alice Perrers, who was accused of a variety of offences – interfering with the courts of justice, embezzling up to £3,000 a year from the Treasury and bringing dishonour and ill-fame on the King – and Richard Lyons, the leading tax-farmer. When Latimer demanded a formal trial, and asked who accused him, de la Mare replied that all of the Commons did so, thus almost by accident stumbling on the deadly weapon of impeachment. Finally, the Commons demanded a reconstruction of the royal Council, to replace members of the Gaunt faction, and the formal swearing of the new Council before Parliament. In return, they granted a wool subsidy, but only for three months. The King did not negotiate these harsh terms; he simply accepted them, adding an old man's plea that Alice should not be treated harshly.

The Commons had, in effect, by the time Parliament broke up on 10 July after its longest session in history, carried through a constitutional revolution, for though the Black Prince and Wykeham were variously thought to be manipulating MPs behind the scenes, the initiative had in fact been taken by the leading knights and merchants of the House. The Black Prince, in any case, was on his deathbed in Westminster Palace, and to the end remained on terms with his brother Gaunt. Wykeham may have been active through his episcopal friends on the bench, but he was too prudent to place himself at the head of a Commons revolt. The likelihood is that de la Mare, and his supporter or patron the Mortimer Earl of March (married to the King's grand-daughter) were the leading spirits. But they lacked both the logic and the appetite of revolutionaries. It was pointless to humiliate Gaunt and the Lancastrian interest unless they were prepared to take the government wholly in their

Richard of Bordeaux, son of the Black Prince and successor to Edward III. He won early popularity for his handling of Wat Tyler's rebellion but was eventually deposed by his cousin Henry of Lancaster, son of John of Gaunt.

hands, and if necessary defend their actions by force. But this was much further than they were willing to go. The Commons did not yet regard itself as an executive instrument, but as a channel for reforms, whose enactment was the responsibility of the King and Council. And, after half a century of constitutional stability, there could be no question of violence while the King lived.

On the other hand, Gaunt had been placed in a position in which he had little alternative but to react vigorously. Terrible rumours were circulating about him – that he was a changeling, smuggled into Ghent Abbey in place of the daughter born to Queen Philippa, that his real father was a butcher, that he was living in sin with his daughters' governess, Katherine Swinford (this was true), that he had poisoned his first wife's sister. Most seriously, he was accused of plotting with the Pope to declare the young Richard of Bordeaux, the Black Prince's surviving son and now heir to the throne, illegitimate, making himself the heir apparent. Parliament had, indeed, taken sufficient cognisance of this last charge to pass an enactment specifically recognising Richard as the heir.

Gaunt thus had to defend himself, and he was tempted also to play the anti-clericalist card. For some years Gaunt had been a patron of John Wyklif, the radical Oxford scholar who had achieved a wide reputation and following by his writings, teaching and preaching on the subject of ecclesiastical abuses. Until the Peasants' Revolt of 1381 shook the confidence of the lay establishment, he enjoyed, indeed, the protection of a powerful group of magnates. His attacks on indulgences, on papal taxation and provisions, on clerical exactions and, above all, on the monastic and mendicant orders, were generally popular, and widely reflected in the polemical literature of the time. Wyklif was Gaunt's answer to the bench of bishops, and in particular to Wykeham, the richest clericalist of all.

In the autumn of 1376, at a great Council held at Westminster, Gaunt reversed the decisions of what was to be called the 'Good Parliament'. De la Mare was put in Nottingham Gaol. March and his supporters lost their offices. Perrers was brought back to Court. Wykeham was charged with abuse of office during his Chancellorship up to 1371, sentenced to forfeiture of his temporalities and forbidden to come within twenty miles of Court. Gaunt followed this up by summoning a Parliament for January 1377, which he had made efforts to pack; its Speaker, Sir John Hungerford, was one of his officials, and the opening sermon was preached by a loyal cleric, the Bishop of St Davids, who declared that the King had recovered his health, though the young heir Richard, now made Prince of Wales, formally presided. Edward had now been on the throne fifty years, and a general amnesty was passed to mark his jubilee. The Commons voted a poll-tax of 4d, but raised difficulties, demanding the release of de la Mare. The bishops, too, refused to vote money until Wykeham was restored to his rights. Indeed, they counter-attacked, by hauling Wyklif before a court of Convocation, and charging him with heresy.

From this arose the final spasm of the reign. Gaunt felt that his credit and reputation rested on his willingness and ability to protect his protégés, as no doubt it did. He not only instructed counsel to defend Wyklif, but went to Convocation with an

William of Wykeham

From humble origins in the village of Wykeham in
Hampshire, William rose through the King's
service to be Lord Chancellor and Bishop of
Winchester. Apart from his work for the King,
including the grand additions to Windsor Castle,
he had three great personal achievements: the
founding of Winchester College and New
College, Oxford, and the rebuilding of the nave of
Winchester Cathedral.

RIGHT The Founder's crozier from New
College.
BELOW The effigy of William of Wykeham in
Winchester Cathedral.
OPPOSITE The nave of Winchester looking west.

armed following and broke up the court, after an angry exchange of abuse with its president, Bishop Courtenay of London. What is more, he let it be known that, by virtue of his office as Marshal, he intended to exercise military law in London. This gave the clericalists – not normally popular in the capital – an excuse to agitate the London mob, and a crowd of many thousands smashed their way into Gaunt's Savoy Palace, reversed his arms – as a symbol of treason – and chased to Westminster servants in his livery. Gaunt fled for his life to Kennington, where the widowed Joan of Wales gave him refuge. There followed long negotiations, during which a political compromise was reached. The Londoners agreed to apologise to Gaunt, depose their mayor and erect a marble column in Cheapside bearing the Lancaster arms. The Duke was further mollified by being awarded palatine powers in his duchy. But Wykeham was restored and de la Mare released. The realm thus achieved an uneasy equipoise, from which it might descend either to constitutional anarchy, or to the tyranny of the executive.

Edward took no part in these events. Indeed he was dying in his palace at Richmond. The political harmony of his reign was dissolved, but he could do nothing to control or unify the factions, other than acquiesce passively in their verdicts. He was not wholly discredited; the echo of his reputation could still invoke a flicker of respect. In the version of *Piers Plowman* which Langland updated in 1377, he compares Edward to a cat, whom an assembly of mice and rats (Parliament) are seeking to bell; but he warns that worse will come when the old cat dies, and the rule of the kitten (Richard II) brings chaos: a prophetic fancy.

The King died on 21 June 1377, after a final stroke. The St Albans chronicler declares that he was left alone at the end, except for his confessor, and that Alice Perrers even stripped him of his finger-rings. This is no doubt an invention: no such charges were ever brought against her in the courts. Gaunt was a faithful son, and saw to it that the obsequies of his father were properly conducted, as befitted an English monarch and a great Christian warrior. On his wife's deathbed, Edward had agreed warmly to her request that he should be buried alongside her in Westminster Abbey, and this was duly carried out. Her own

PREVIOUS PAGES The effigy of Edward III in Westminster Abbey.

matronly image was already installed. In accordance with custom, a wooden effigy of the King, dressed and painted as in life, was placed on his bier during the funeral procession. Its face, which has survived, was evidently done from a death-mask, since one side of the mouth is twisted with paralysis. But for the effigy on the monument itself, cast in bronze, the marks of pain and weakness were smoothed out. The King is shown as an old man, his long hair and beard falling in graceful folds around a face which radiates serenity and benevolence. It is, of course, an artistic eulogy, a panegyric in metal which ignores the tragedies of his last decade, and presents an elder statesman and retired general not as he was, but as he might and should have been. This is no more than justice. Though Edward lived too long for his reputation, the cruelty of age could not wholly efface his achievements. His victories proved ephemeral, but they bought time. He maintained the consensus of the realm over many decades, through war and natural disaster and unprecedented social change, allowing its institutions to grow and its sense of unity to mature. It could be said: he inherited a kingdom; he bequeathed a nation.

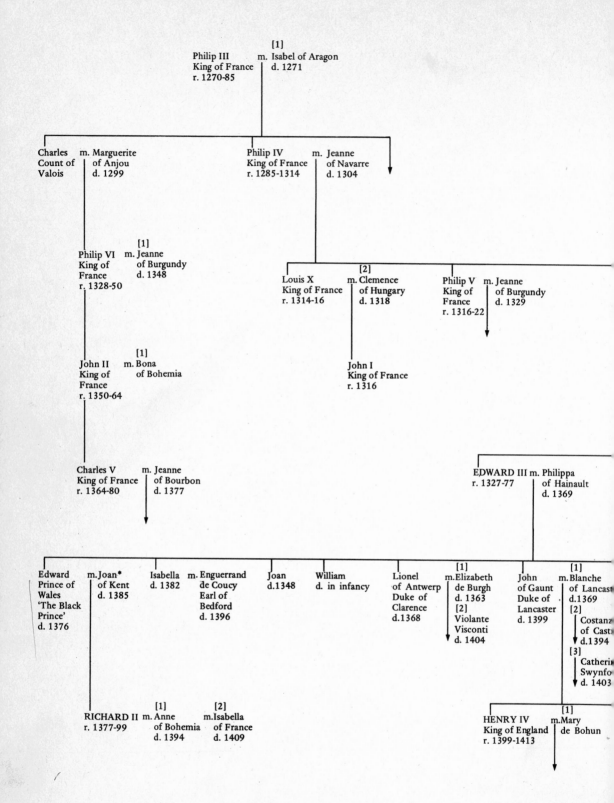

[1]
Philip III   m. Isabel of Aragon
King of France   d. 1271
r. 1270-85

Charles   m. Marguerite   Philip IV   m. Jeanne
Count of   of Anjou   King of France   of Navarre
Valois   d. 1299   r. 1285-1314   d. 1304

                [1]
Philip VI   m. Jeanne   [2]
King of   of Burgundy   Louis X   m. Clemence   Philip V   m. Jeanne
France   d. 1348   King of France of Hungary   King of   of Burgundy
r. 1328-50   r. 1314-16   d. 1318   France   d. 1329
                                                              r. 1316-22

                [1]
John II   m. Bona   John I
King of   of Bohemia   King of France
France   r. 1316
r. 1350-64

Charles V   m. Jeanne   EDWARD III m. Philippa
King of France of Bourbon   r. 1327-77   of Hainault
r. 1364-80   d. 1377   d. 1369

                                                                    [1]   [1]
Edward   m.Joan*   Isabella m. Enguerrand Joan   William   Lionel   m.Elizabeth   John   m.Blanche
Prince of   of Kent   d. 1382   de Coucy   d.1348   d. in   of Antwerp de Burgh   of Gaunt   of Lancast
Wales   d. 1385   Earl of   infancy   Duke of   d. 1363   Duke of   d.1369
'The Black   Bedford   Clarence   [2]   Lancaster [2]
Prince'   d. 1396   d.1368   Violante   d. 1399   Costanz
d. 1376   Visconti   of Cast
                                                                                    d. 1404   d.1394
                                                                                                             [3]
                                                                                                               Catheri
                                                                                                               Swynfo
                                                                                                               d. 1403

                [1]   [2]   [1]
RICHARD II   m. Anne   m.Isabella   HENRY IV   m.Mary
r. 1377-99   of Bohemia   of France   King of England de Bohun
             d. 1394   d. 1409   r. 1399-1413

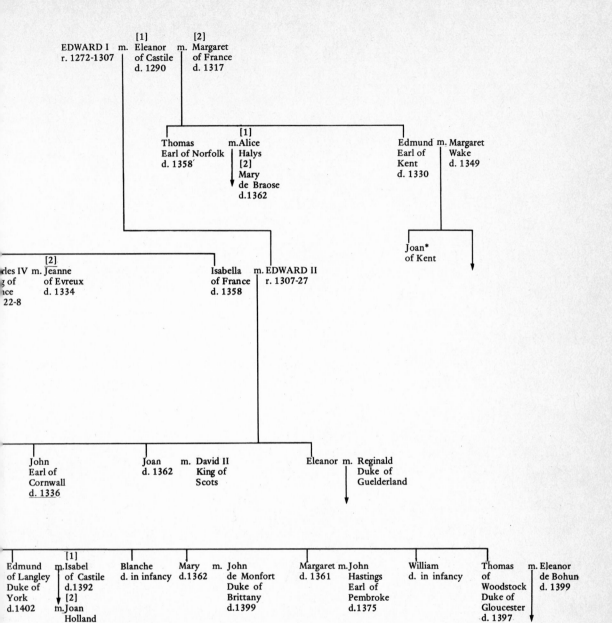

EDWARD I m. Eleanor m. Margaret
r. 1272-1307 of Castile of France
d. 1290 d. 1317

[1] [2]

Thomas m.Alice Edmund m. Margaret
Earl of Norfolk Halys Earl of Wake
d. 1358 [2] Kent d. 1349
Mary d. 1330
de Braose
d.1362

Joan*
of Kent

[2]
les IV m. Jeanne Isabella m. EDWARD II
g of of Evreux of France r. 1307-27
nce d. 1334 d. 1358
22-8

John Joan m. David II Eleanor m. Reginald
Earl of d. 1362 King of Duke of
Cornwall Scots Guelderland
d. 1336

Edmund m.Isabel Blanche Mary m. John Margaret m.John William Thomas m. Eleanor
of Langley of Castile d. in infancy d.1362 de Monfort d. 1361 Hastings d. in infancy of de Bohun
Duke of d.1392 Duke of Earl of Woodstock d. 1399
York [2] Brittany Pembroke Duke of
d.1402 m.Joan d.1399 d.1375 Gloucester
Holland d. 1397
d.1434

Select bibliography

The best general introduction to the reign is May McKisack, *The Fourteenth Century* (Oxford, 1959), which has a full bibliography. A wide selection of extracts from the sources is printed in A.R. Myers, *English Historical Documents IV 1327-1485* (London, 1969).

Of the chronicles, the most important are: Adam of Murimuth, *Continuatio Chronicorum* (ed. E.M. Thompson, Rolls Series, 1889); Geoffrey de Baker, *Chronicon* (ed. E.M. Thompson, Oxford, 1889); Bridlington, *Gesta Edwardi de Caernarvon* (ed. Bishop Stubbs, Rolls Series, 1882-3); Lanercost, *Chronicle* (ed. J. Stevenson, Edinburgh, 1839); Thomas Walsingham, *Chronicon Angliae* (ed. E.M. Thompson, Rolls Series, 1874); Henry Knighton, *Chronicon* (ed. J.R. Lumby, Rolls Series, 1889-95); the *Anonimalle Chronicle* (ed. V.H. Galbraith, Manchester, 1927); Ranulf Higden, *Polychronicon* (ed. J.R. Lumby, Rolls Series, 1889); the Chandos Herald, *Life of the Black Prince* (translated and ed. M.K. Pope and E.C. Lodge, London, 1910); Jean Froissart, *Chronicle*, available in many editions; and Jean le Bel, *Chronicle* (ed. J. Viard and E. Déprez, Paris, 1904-5).

There is no good modern biography of Edward III; of older works, the best are: Joshua Barnes, *History of Edward III* (Cambridge, 1688); W. Longman, *Life and Times of Edward III* (London, 1869); and J. Mackinnon: *History of Edward III* (London, 1900). Other relevant biographical studies include: Harold F. Hutchison, *Edward II, the Pliant King* (London, 1971); K.A. Fowler, *The King's Lieutenant: Henry of Grosmont* (London, 1969); S. Armitage Smith, *John of Gaunt* (London, 1904); K.B. McFarlane, *John Wycliffe and the Beginnings of English Nonconformity* (London, 1952).

For the Hundred Years' War, the most useful modern summary is: Kenneth Fowler (ed.), *The Hundred Years' War* (London, 1971); other studies include E. Perroy, *The Hundred Years' War* (English trans. 1951); H.J. Hewitt, *The Organisation of War under Edward III* (Manchester, 1966); M.H. Keen, *The Laws of War in the Late Middle Ages* (Oxford, 1965); and P.E. Russell, *The English Intervention in Spain and Portugal in the Time of Edward III and Richard II* (Oxford, 1955). The impact of the war on the structure of English society is discussed in K.B. McFarlane: *The Nobility of Later Medieval England* (Oxford, 1973).

A number of important articles on Parliament in the fourteenth century are collected in E.B.Fryde and Edward Miller (eds.), *Historical Studies of the English Parliament, i: Origins to 1399* (Cambridge, 1970); the *Modus Tenendi Parliamentum* is published in J.J. Bagley and P.B.Rowley, *A Documentary History of England, i: 1066-1540* (London, 1966). T.F.Tout's *Chapters in the Administrative History of Medieval England* (Manchester, 1920–33) is still the best survey of government under Edward III; see also E.B.Fryde, 'Materials for the Study of Edward III's Credit Operations 1327-48', *Bulletin of the Institute of Historical Research* 22-3 (1949-50).

For cultural, religious and social affairs, the following are particularly useful: H.M.Colvin (ed.), *The History of the King's Works, Vols i-iii* (London, 1964); B.Cottle, *The Triumph of English* (London, 1969); *The Holkham Bible Picture Book*, W.D.Hassall (ed.) (London, 1954); Gervase Mathew, *The Court of Richard II* (London, 1968); Philip Ziegler, *The Black Death* (London, 1969); Joan Evans, *English Art 1307-1461* (Oxford, 1949); Margaret Wood, *The English Medieval House* (London, 1965); Maurice Beresford and John G.Hurst, *Deserted Medieval Villages* (London, 1971); Maurice Beresford, *New Towns in England and Wales* (London, 1967); R.R.Tighe and J.E. Davis, *Annals of Windsor, i* (London, 1858); Martin M.Crow and Clair C.Olson (eds.), *Chaucer Life Records*; Violet Pritchard, *English Medieval Graffiti* (Cambridge, 1967); Lawrence Stone, *Sculpture in Britain in the Middle Ages* (London, 1955); Geoffrey Webb, *Architecture in Britain: The Middle Ages* (London, 1956); E.W.Tristram, *English Wall Painting of the 14th Century* (London, 1955); M.Rickert, *Painting in Britain: The Middle Ages* (London, 1954); E.K.Chambers, *The Medieval Stage* (Oxford, 1903); Glynne Wickham, *Early English Stages, i 1300-1576* (London, 1959); Percy M.Young, *A History of British Music* (London, 1967); Francis W.Galpin, *Old English Instruments of Music* (4th ed. London, 1965); Lord Twining, *A History of the Crown Jewels of Europe* (London, 1960); A.Hamilton Thompson, *The English Clergy and their Organisation in the later Middle Ages* (Oxford, 1947); David Knowles, *The Religious Orders in England, ii* (Cambridge, 1955); K.L.Wood-Legh, *Studies in Church Life in England under Edward III* (London, 1934). A useful introduction to the literature of the period is Kenneth Sisam (ed.), *Fourteenth-Century Verse and Prose* (Oxford, 1950).

Index